THE 4 A.M.
BREAKTHROUGH

THE 4 A.M.
BREAKTHROUGH

UNCONVENTIONAL WRITING EXERCISES
THAT TRANSFORM YOUR FICTION

BRIAN KITELEY

WRITER'S
DIGEST
BOOKS

WRITER'S DIGEST BOOKS

An imprint of Penguin Random House LLC
penguinrandomhouse.com

Copyright © 2008 by Brian Kiteley
Penguin supports copyright. Copyright fuels creativity, encourages diverse
voices, promotes free speech, and creates a vibrant culture. Thank you for
buying an authorized edition of this book and for complying with copyright
laws by not reproducing, scanning, or distributing any part of it in any form
without permission. You are supporting writers and allowing Penguin
to continue to publish books for every reader.

Robert Creeley's "I Know a Man," from *The Collected Poems of Robert Creeley, 1945-1975*,
reprinted with permission of University of California Press and the Estate of Robert Creeley.

Library of Congress Cataloging-in-Publication Data

Kiteley, Brian.

The 4 a.m. breakthrough : unconventional writing exercises that transform your fiction / by
Brian Kiteley. -- 1st ed.

p. cm.

Includes index.

ISBN 978-1-58297-563-4 (pbk. : alk. paper)

1. Fiction--Authorship. 2. Fiction--Technique--Problems, exercises, etc. I. Title. II. Title:
Four a.m. breakthrough.

PN3355.K54 2008

808.3--dc28

Edited by Lauren Mosko
Designed by Claudean Wheeler, based on a design by Grace Ring

146122990

DEDICATION

For my parents, Murray and Jean Kiteley

ACKNOWLEDGMENTS

I wish to thank to Janet Bland, Cynthia Coburn, Ann Dobyns, Andrea Dupree, Brian Evenson, Jane Friedman, T.J. Gerlach, Eli Gottlieb, Joanna Howard, Laird Hunt, Eric Melbye, Erin Morrill, Lauren Mosko, Lance Olsen, Amanda Rea, Selah Saterstrom, and Robert Urquhart.

Parts of this book have appeared in different form in Michael Martone's *Rules of Thumb*, Sherry Ellis's *Now Write*, Steve Earnshaw's *The Handbook of Creative Writing*, and an issue of *McSweeney's* edited by Justin Taylor.

My home page is www.du.edu/~bkiteley. I will answer questions and clarify the exercises over the coming months and years on those pages. I would be most interested to hear how the exercises work, and which exercises don't work (or don't make sense).

TABLE OF CONTENTS

THE BASICS

WHAT YOU NEED TO KNOW 002

THE EXERCISES

PATTERNS 029

029 STYLE

1 Parataxis, 2 Paragraphs as Containers, 3 Etymologies, 4 Language Is Always an Abbreviation, 5 The Letter A, 6 The Letter B, 7 Potholes, 8 Rhetorical Questions, 9 Essay Fiction

040 USED LITERATURE

10 Sorrow-Acre, 11 Your Swann, 12 The Systems Novel, 13 Big Two-Hearted River, 14 A Canticle for Leibowitz, 15 Ihab Hassan, 16 Bruno Schulz, 17 Isaac Babel, 18 No Time, 19 Grace Paley, 20 Palimpsest, 21 Robert Creeley, 22 Poetry & England

059 OLD AND NEW MEDIA

23 MapQuest, 24 Oddvertising, 25 Public Art, 26 My Neighbor Totoro, 27 Reruns, 28 The Pinup, 29 The Shouting Phase of Sitcoms, 30 Blogs, 31 Old News, 32 Lies of the Press, 33 The Happy Boy and His Family, 34 Headless Body in Topless Bar, 35 The Devious Lie of a Snapshot, 36 The Party, 37 Son of a Preacher Man, 38 Beverly Sills, 39 The Concept Album

079 LANGUAGE GAMES

40 Anagrams, 41 Concordance, 42 Encyclopedias, 43 250
Different Words, 44 Recuperation, 45 Translation
From the Same Language, 46 Substitution, 47 Index,
48 Automatic Writing, 49 Weekly Exercise

090 ALGORITHMS

50 Fact and Fancy Reversed, 51 No Middle, Two
Endings, 52 Aphorisms, 53 Country Noises,
54 Coincidence, 55 Recycling, 56 Machine in the
Garden, 57 Philosophy and Its Discontents

CONCEPTS **101**

101 LOVE & LUST

58 Song of Songs, 59 The Carnal & the Domestic,
60 The Three Stooges, 61 Siding With the Father,
62 Beauty & Lust, 63 Love & Chance, 64 Symbiosis,
65 Addicted to Love, 66 Striptease, 67 The Hotel
Bed, 68 Serendipity, 69 Pillow Talk, 70 Divorce Sex,
71 Love E-mails

115 THE MIND

72 The Insistence on Meaning, 73 Buzzing Blooming
Confusion, 74 Information Sickness, 75 On Hashish,
76 Learning to See, 77 Blind, 78 Multilingual, 79 Autism,
80 Narcissism, 81 Driving, 82 Numerical Cognition

130   EMOTION

83 Pain, 84 Hiding Emotions, 85 Redness, 86 Grief,
87 Enjoy the Process, 88 Laughter Is How We Connect,
89 Sobbing, 90 The Collector of Injustices, 91 Selective
Mutism, 92 We Think With the Objects We Love,
93 A Curse

141   DEATH

94 Obituary, 95 Imagine Your Own Death, 96 Near
Death, 97 9/11, 98 Falling Out of the Sky, 99 Carrying
a Body, 100 The Coma, 101 A Massacre, 102 Xenophobia,
103 Killing the Parents, 104 The Fun in Funeral,
105 Dying Young

153   RELIGION

106 Private Prayer, 107 American Ramadan, 108 The
Devil's Holiday, 109 The Priest, 110 The Apocalypse,
111 The Watchtower, 112 An American in Mecca,
113 Unbelievers Exit Here, 114 Ritual & Disorder

162   SCIENCE

115 Retinal Ennui, 116 Camouflage, 117 Perfect
Weather, 118 UFO, 119 That's Life, 120 Smell Is
Emotional, 121 The Tarantula Hawk

169   POLITICS

122 What Democracy Means to Me, 123 One Shit at a
Time, 124 The Negative Master Narrative, 125 Doubt,
126 Republicans, 127 War Stories, 128 Good & Evil

178 JOKES

129 Meta-humor, 130 Guy Walks Into a Bar, 131 A
Practical Joke, 132 Controlled Incongruity, 133 The
Impressionist, 134 He's Had Enough, 135 Cartoon
Texts, 136 Comic Balloons, 137 Straight Man

187 HISTORY

138 The Story of a Year, 139 After Auschwitz,
140 Eunuch, 141 The Dust Bowl, 142 History
& Fiction, 143 History as Literary Looting,
144 Christmas Every Three Months, 145 CBGB

PEOPLE, PLACES, THINGS 198

198 CHARACTER VS. CARICATURE

146 A Prospero Figure, 147 Wallace & Gromit,
148 Flâneur, 149 A Beautiful Woman, 150 The Fiction
Writer & the Lawyer, 151 Ambition, 152 Self-Loathing,
153 Close Talker, 154 Costumes, 155 Fruitfulness I.
Kippers, 156 Rejuveniles

208 VOICES & TALK

157 A Burglar Smoking a Fine Cigar, 158 Fractured
Fairy Tale, 159 Plants, 160 Unbelieving, 161 Trialogue,
162 A Car Wreck in Repose, 163 Therapeutic Lying,
164 Donald Rumsfeld, 165 Dressing Up

216   FAMILY & FRIENDS

166 Parents as Two Continents, 167 Thanksgivings,
168 Brothers, 169 Sisters, 170 Birth Order,
171 Abandonment, 172 Child Abuse, 173 Friendships
of the Good, 174 Friendship's End, 175 Our Pets,
176 The Letter in the Desk

228   EDUCATION & SCHOOL

177 College, 178 Among Schoolchildren, 179 The Jean
Cocteau Repertory, 180 Prep School, 181 Daydreams,
182 Boys & Girls, 183 Mirroring

235   PLACE

184 Mythologizing Home, 185 Biggar, 186 The
United States & Canada, 187 A U.S. Town, 188 Lost,
189 Biography of a Country, 190 Naked City

242   FOOD & DRINK

191 Abalone, 192 Alcohol, 193 Bacon in Egypt,
194 Lobster Bisque

248   MONEY & CLASS

195 Swearing, 196 The Corporation vs. the
Individual, 197 Money, 198 Class Dismissed,
199 The Camp, 200 Marlon Brando

THE APPENDICES

255   A. MY REFERENCE BOOKS

258   B. ADVICE FOR TEACHERS AND STUDENTS

265   C. A CONVERSATION ABOUT
      TEACHING FICTION EXERCISES

271   EXERCISE INDEX

THE
BASICS

WHAT YOU NEED TO KNOW

This book is a companion to *The 3 A.M. Epiphany*. The two books
work in tandem, but you can also read *The 4 A.M. Breakthrough*
by itself. In this book I give much less basic fiction writing advice than I gave in *The 3 A.M. Epiphany* (which came mostly in
the introductions to the chapters). Here I jump right into the problems and processes of these two hundred exercises. The exercises
should speak for themselves. The categories of exercises in *The
4 A.M. Breakthrough* are, with one or two exceptions, new. The
Appendix has advice on how to teach this book.

MY HISTORY WITH FICTION EXERCISES

Accidental exercises. The first decent story I wrote began as a combination of two different exercises. I'd been writing the same kind
of mediocre story for six years. In 1982, I wrote in my journal an
imitation of Thomas Pynchon because I was reading and thorough-
ly enjoying his first novel, *V.* In the same journal, I wrote another
imitation (of Evelyn Waugh, who several months later fascinated
me). I wrote it on a blank page in the journal, as it happened right
next to the Pynchon imitation, because by accident I'd left two
pages in the journal blank and then moved on. This was obviously
not a conscious act. I opened to those blank pages and started
writing the imitation of Waugh, thinking I was writing it in the
proper place in the journal. In fact, I wrote it several months behind the current entries. I noticed the mistake only when I turned
the page to continue the exercise, and discovered I was writing
in the "past" of the journal. Then I looked at the exercise on the

previous page and realized both pieces of fiction were about the town in southern Spain where my family lived for three months in 1969 when I was thirteen. I liked the way the two stories fit together, even though they had very different sets of characters. I had not intended for the two stories to go together, but it was easy enough to link them because of the shared town, Nerja. One was about a young British woman who'd just killed her Spanish boyfriend (maybe in self-defense) and the other story was about my brother and our family. For a long time afterward I was very conscious of the fact that an accident triggered the first really good fiction I wrote. In effect, I used a fiction exercise to create my first good story. I knew I was writing an exercise by imitating Pynchon and Waugh, but the second part of the exercise was the accident and the real revelation—to combine such apparently unrelated parts to make a different whole.

Language is alive. On my home page at the University of Denver (www.du.edu/~bkiteley), I wrote this sentence years ago: "I believe language is infinitely malleable, a live being in our hands, which deserves our great respect and curiosity." One exercise I designed for *The 3 A.M. Epiphany* (and have used myself several times) is to take the full name of someone you love and use the letters from that name as the only alphabet available for a set of words and sentences that serve as the raw material for a very short piece of narrative. I did this using my brother's name. My brother died of AIDS in 1993, and I'd been trying for years to compose my thoughts about him. The page of fiction that grew out of this

exercise was a construction of the last moments—and thoughts—
of his life. The story took several years to write (even though it was
never much more than a page long), which seemed like a natural
amount of work for a project about my brother's last thoughts. The
way these sentences—and this language—came to me, in laborious and methodical pieces, is an example of how one can reflect
on language—words and letters even—in a microscopic way, not
seeing narrative of any sort but seeing the most basic elements
of fiction. The vignette arranges and rearranges the words I could
come up with from a set of SCRABBLE letters (literally) scattered
around my desk. I had to seek out the only words available to me
in this arbitrary fashion, yet I also saw how much my mind was
still manipulating the material without the more conscious part of
my mind knowing it. This is a good example of what I mean when
I say language is a live being in our hands.

EQUIVALENT PROCESSES

Adapt, improvise, and overcome. Former baseball player and manager Yogi Berra said, "You can't think and hit at the same time."
But can you think and write at the same time? Writers should
practice hard, work on repetitions, and think through the process
as much as they can, whatever the process is. But when it comes
to actual competition—writing the fiction itself, like playing ten-
nis or golf—writers should trust that they have trained their instincts well and not think at all. Practice makes for better instincts.
Fiction exercises are one part of a very particular sort of practice

to build better instincts. There has always been a practical, in-
structional attitude in American fiction—it often dismisses opinion and interpretation. There has also been an ideal of the naïve
innocent, the rube who came to the city from the farm and wrote
down great stories about driving an ambulance in a war. American
fiction writers, much more than European or Latin American fiction writers, like this notion of the conversational, easy, unprac-
ticed, apparently guileless novel or story. The Marines have a
saying, "Adapt, improvise, and overcome." Writing fiction is not
like going into battle, but you do test yourself the way a soldier
tests himself. The first two commands—*adapt* and *improvise*—are
crucial. Writing fiction is somewhat like living reality—it is unpredictable, but you can train yourself to react gracefully to life's
surprises. Prepare for fiction the way soldiers train for battle.

Staying one step ahead of disaster. The filmmaker Orson Welles
said, "[The director's] job is to preside over accidents." In *The
3 A.M. Epiphany* I quoted Daniel Dennett, in *Consciousness
Explained*, who theorized that the task of the human brain "is to
guide the body it controls through a world of shifting conditions
and sudden surprises, [to] ... gather information from that world
and use it swiftly to 'produce future'—to extract anticipations in
order to stay one step ahead of disaster." We read fiction to see
how characters improvise their lives moment by moment to survive. In order to write fiction, we need to train to build up and
stretch certain muscles and practice a variety of plans for retreat
or attack. We practice our skills at improvisation, which sounds

like a contradiction in terms, but it isn't. Actors who specialize in improvisation do not do a typical rehearsal by reading lines. They practice by responding to phrases, props, or new costumes thrown at them. They have to react without any preparation or even thinking.

One of my role models as a teacher is Harry Mathews, author of *My Life in CIA*. Harry's approach to fiction workshops is closer to an acting class than a typical writing class. Over the course of a couple of hours he would inspire students to take on different parts of a fictional persona, actually adopting layers of a self, as an improv actor would. This persona might or might not become a narrator or a character in the student's fiction. I once took a one-day workshop with Harry (which he insisted should be eight hours long) when he visited the University of Denver. He staggered the parts of the exercises, interleaving them, so we were not always sure which exercises we were doing. He made us act out our possible characters, speaking aloud their quirks and endearing insanities. Harry also showed me, more than any other writer, how one can play with form and restraint to make beautiful music out of the essential structures of fiction.

Learn by doing. In the early 1980s, Sid Caesar was a guest host of *Saturday Night Live*, during the down years when Lorne Michaels was not producing the show. Caesar was host of his own similar show in the 1950s, *Your Show of Shows*, and he was amazed by the way the *SNL* writers proposed their sketches each week before the Saturday show. They gathered twenty or thirty sketches, partly written and even rehearsed a little bit. Caesar said they were wasting a great deal of time on each of these sketches. In his show the writers proposed a sketch with a line of description, not much more. If the sketch was accepted for the show, the line was turned slowly into a whole playlet (or sketch), and the thing was worked on until it was funny, right, and perfect. But *SNL* operated with the notion of looking at these thirty or so rounded-out sketches, even though it seemed to waste a lot of the writers' time.

What intrigues me about this story is that these writers were operating on something like the system of fiction exercises I advocate in this book and in *The 3 A.M. Epiphany*. They wrote whole small pieces instead of a brief outline form of the idea. I propose an alternative to the idea of outlining a story or novel. I have never written outlines for my fiction. My novels have had very simple structures—an entomologist's field notes or an aimless walk through Cairo that two men take during Ramadan. I believe in learning by doing, like building an airplane in the air. Because of my novels' uncomplicated outlines, I feel free to include whatever catches my eye during a day's composition. These exercises are a formal way of filtering the day's residue.

Never throw out sketches. The apparent excess of the *Saturday Night Live* system allows writers to work out stories and sketches over long periods of time. Perhaps in *Your Show of Shows* the writers did keep track of ideas for future sketches as they were working on the week's sketches. But what *SNL* seems to have perfected is the notion of an ongoing, endlessly revisable file of stories. The writers hone their stories, working on them week after week until perhaps one week the sketch catches the producers' fancies.

One year, Larry David was a writer on *SNL* (several years before he began coproducing his own sitcom, *Seinfeld*). He wrote dozens of sketches, only three of which made it to the show itself. One of the actors he frequently used in these proposed sketches was Julia Louis-Dreyfus. The sketches he wrote for her were revived when it came time to write the plots of *Seinfeld*. The reason they were rejected by Lorne Michaels, apparently, was that they were generally about nothing, merely acutely observed descriptions of ordinary life (which sounds a lot like what *Seinfeld* became). The moral of this story is that you should not throw anything out. Think of your writing as a collection of rough drafts. Do fiction exercises for whatever you're working on, but also just as play, practice, to keep writing when nothing feels inspiring. Organize your exercises, put them in groups with other similar pieces, rewrite their titles often, reread them, and reorganize them.

Schmucks with laptops. Jack Warner, the Hollywood mogul from the first half of the twentieth century, dismissively called his screenwriters "schmucks with Underwoods," which were the most common typewriters of the day. The full quote is, "Actors? Schmucks. Screenwriters? Schmucks with Underwoods." We are all schmucks with Underwoods or laptop computers—we're all in this game for the love of the game, not the money. No one else cares if we write or don't write. This book aims at demystifying the process of writing. These exercises should make you realize it is possible—and even fun—to write fiction. Lao Tze's maxim that each long journey begins with one step is something like what I'm trying to teach with this book and with *The 3 A.M. Epiphany*. Each exercise is a step. Make enough of them and let them interlock and interact, and you have a short story, a novel, or a long hike into the wilderness of your imagination. Your stories don't have to be made up entirely of exercises, but if you become stuck, try one or two. Give yourself many options. If you're stalled and you have several choices to make about a possible scene or section of writing, it will be easier to proceed. It is much harder to resolve your dilemmas when you have no alternatives.

EXPERIMENTS & FICTION

Showing evidence of its own making. My ideal story or novel reveals the history of its own making, as well as all the other things a story or novel should do. I don't mean metafiction, which is a story told by the author who appears in the story (that "author" becomes a character in the book, not necessarily the author of the book). All books contain details of the histories of their making, but some writers can't help exposing those details more plainly than other writers. Why do I like novels that show their own constructions? Eighteenth- and nineteenth-century novels had lists of contents at the beginning of each chapter ("in which the hero makes a fool of himself over a cup of coffee") and sometimes running heads at the top of each page that described what was happening in that page, for the purpose of keeping the reader informed and perhaps allowing the reader to luxuriate in the details of the moment being described. Donald Barthelme's story "Paraguay" starts with a quotation from another writer writing not about Paraguay but Tibet, which is noted only in a footnote at the end of this quoted paragraph. The reader reads along feeling the odd style, noting the archaic tone, but at ease and at home in this imagined country of "Paraguay." The footnote is at the bottom of the second page, a crucial delay of recognition I'm sure Barthelme worked out typologically. It tells us that all travel in a very foreign place is similar, even interchangeable; it revokes our reality, too. A reader skipping past the footnote will not know that Barthelme has been playing with the way descriptions of foreign places blur into one another.

No drinking over Kansas. In 1970, the Attorney General of Kansas tried to prevent airlines from serving alcohol while flying over his state, which did not allow the sale of any alcohol at the time. This sort of quixotic historical fact often makes fiction look strangely pale and unimaginative compared to the peculiarities and (sometimes) sheer unbelievability of reality. Sprinkle in this kind of historical or contemporary reality liberally with your own fictionalizing. There is and should be no real difference between fiction and nonfiction. The distinction between the fictional and the fact-based world is overrated and the distance between the two is shorter than most critics imagine.

Self-conscious games. Michiko Kakutani, a regular book reviewer for the *New York Times*, said of Dave Eggers, "[he] is a writer torn between two warring proclivities: a taste for the latest postmodern, self-conscious literary games and an ability to write genuinely moving, heartfelt narratives about real people and their very real lives." Why are these two things necessarily at war—in Dave Eggers or in anyone—these days? I was a student of Donald Barthelme, who did both of these "warring" things with a great deal of grace and intelligence. I think many writers do both—write playful, allusive, intelligent, heartfelt fiction. Look at Clifford Chase's book *Winkie*, about his teddy bear, which had been his mother's teddy bear before that, and later on was brought to life by some obscure desire, then confused for a terrorist by our idiotic federal government. Chase's book is sincere autobiography, weird adult fairy tale, and a serious study of an animated teddy bear baffled by the modern world. Play is a solemn and integral part of life, and adult versions of childhood fantasies can be both self-conscious and genuinely moving.

Hysterical realism. I've always objected to this phrase, which the great but conservative book reviewer James Wood coined to describe postmodern fiction. It uses a sexist word, *hysterical*, which is falling out of use these days; it came from the Greek word *hysterikos*, meaning "of the womb," and *hysteria* was defined as a neurotic condition peculiar to women and thought to be caused by a dysfunction of the uterus. Below is a long excerpt of Stephen Marche's obituary of the French writer Alain

Robbe-Grillet (who coined the term *Nouveau Roman* [the new novel]), from *Salon*, March 6, 2008, in which he takes on just these issues very nicely:

> It is entirely appropriate that six months before Robbe-Grillet died, James Wood became the principal literary critic at *The New Yorker*. [Wood] is the master and commander of the forces of archaism ... At the core of Wood's appeal as a critic is not an idea or a program but a prejudice, a leaning, that the novel is essentially a nineteenth-century form ... There is more than a faint tinge of moralism in his nostalgia: You should not want to recognize yourself in novels because characters like you are not fit for them. Wood has made himself the opposite of Robbe-Grillet. He instructs us in the maxim "make it old." The novel is not for novelty. Must you show off?
>
> The two brands of Puritanism embodied by Wood and Robbe-Grillet are beginning to crack. Eight years after Wood coined the phrase "hysterical realism," the book of the year [2007] was Junot Díaz's *The Brief Wondrous Life of Oscar Wao*, a perfect example of all he rejected. Robbe-Grillet would have disliked it as well: too much plot and funny dialogue, too many political ideas and witty asides. Writers like Jonathan Safran Foer and David Mitchell, among others, are becoming more aggressive stylistically, and more popular, and more pleasurable.
>
> The two strands of postwar literary fiction, the ultra-radical and the willfully archaic, are both antithetical to the

spirit of the novel itself, which is polyglot and unpredictable. Novels are supposed to be messy. They are written to express ideals and to make money; they steal from everything and everyone—high, middle, and low—belonging to everyone and no one in the same moment. They don't fit anyone's conception. That's why we love them.

Sincerity is in. And here is Scott Turow, reviewing a novel by the very good writer Tony Earley in the *New York Times Book Review*, March 9, 2008, showing exactly what Stephen Marche describes above (pointing out the *Times*'s conservatism, not Tony Earley's):

> Sincerity is in. Never mind the skewering irony of the Facebook generation, or the postmodernism that led boomer intellectuals to see the fractures in every value system. Since 9/11, American readers have shown an appetite for simple tales told with becoming directness. While that approach may never characterize our most self-important fiction, it has been reflected in a number of artful works of popular literature in the last few years.

The key phrase here is "self-important fiction." Turow is a good writer, but he comes from the profession of the law. He might find the notion of writing about the world without his lawyer's experience intimidating (or not what his audience expects). But I have to ask, what is self-important fiction? Is it fiction that takes itself too seriously? I'll grant that self-serious fiction is not a good thing.

But Melville's *Moby-Dick*, Joyce's *Ulysses*, and Barthelme's *The Dead Father* are pretty self-important novels—yet they are also very funny.

Deep play. In *The Interpretation of Cultures*, anthropologist Clifford Geertz defines this odd term (*deep play* sounds like a contradiction in terms: serious play):

> Jeremy Bentham's concept of "deep play" is found in his *The Theory of Legislation*. By it he means play in which the stakes are so high that it is, from his utilitarian standpoint, irrational for men to engage in it at all. If a man whose fortune is a thousand pounds wagers five hundred of it on an even bet, the marginal utility of the pound he stands to win is clearly less than the marginal disutility of the one he stands to lose ... Having come together in search of pleasure [both participants] have entered into a relationship which will bring the participants, considered collectively, net pain rather than net pleasures.

I've always taken deep play to mean a complete engagement in the process, as if there were no outside, nothing beyond the game. Diane Ackerman, in her book *Deep Play*, says, "D.W. Winnicott wrote about play as a creative state of withdrawal from everyday life." Here are some more of Ackerman's insights on the subject, from *Deep Play*:

> Animals play, in part, to stay active and fit. The exploring play of primates helps them gather information about their envi-

ronment and food sources. The escape play of horses keeps them in shape for flight. Social play establishes rank, mate-finding, and cooperation when needed. Play probably helps to keep an animal's senses well informed and alert. The central nervous system needs a certain amount of stimulation. To a dynamic organism, monotony is unbearable. Young animals don't know what is important, what can be safely ignored; they have had fewer novel experiences, and their senses are fresh and highly sensitive. Everything matters.

Old-fashioned innovations. Any fiction that does not observe the fairly strict rules laid down for popular fiction tends to be ignored by major American reviews of books. But innovations that creep into the mainstream become traditions. Multiple perspectives, streams of consciousness, cutting back and forth in time, or even telling stories backwards—these were all radical innovations even fifty years ago. Only the press (the *New York Times Book Review*, for example) and mainstream publishers worry about annoying readers with too much innovation or difficulty. Look at television commercials, TV shows, and big-budget Hollywood movies, and you will see a dizzying array of "experiments" in narrative structure and efficiency.

Christopher Nolan's movie *Memento* (2000) works backwards. Its protagonist has suffered severe short-term memory loss, and he tattoos himself with the information he learns to solve the mystery at the center of the film. This sort of story would have upset audiences and critics alike in 1980, but something has changed in audience expectations. Gradually these innovations in form become familiar and necessary because they describe the chaotic nature of contemporary reality.

Our minds have changed in the last few decades, too. This is obvious to me, as a teacher of twenty-year-olds. The young now especially see the world visually, in a much different way than my generation of baby boomers does. Icons, layers of images on computer screens and TV, multiple uses of attention—these are some of the triggers of the great change in consciousness. This is neither a good nor a bad thing. I have thought, often fruitlessly, about how to engage young readers and writers in my classes. This book and *The 3 A.M. Epiphany* are my attempts to get at these new ways of assembling and comprehending the world.

OTHER ARTS

Duck Amuck. Suspension of disbelief is what happens when a reader of fiction agrees to temporarily suspend his judgment in exchange for the promise of entertainment. The old argument was that if you thought you were reading a piece of fiction, the fiction could not be properly experienced or was not effective as fiction. Suspension of disbelief is more or less a double negative of belief, which is the foundation of the essay and personal nonfiction. In a personal essay, belief is the key. Who believes you, as author? Why do readers believe you? What and when did you start or stop believing certain tenets and golden rules? Life is a series of moments of sudden or gradual believing or disbelieving.

Letters written in the eighteenth century were always meant to be spoken aloud—recited. Only parts specifically directed to one person were read silently. Letters were a communal experience. Silent reading was a later development. Do we actually read fiction as if it were a dream and we were living alongside the characters experiencing the fictional world? Occasionally in film we have an actor turn to the camera and wink. The television show *The Office* (both the British and American versions) operates with the characters (or actors) explicitly aware of the camera. We know we're reading a book we hold in our hands, yet we can still live with the slight conundrum that what we're reading is both happening and also simply on the page. Too much self-awareness, like some of the old-fashioned metafiction practiced in the 1960s and 1970s, can be annoying, but a certain amount of it has crept into our consciousness of the media we watch and enjoy. As long ago as the Bugs Bunny cartoons of the 1940s, the "actors" occasionally turned to the camera and spoke to the audience. The great moment came in *Duck Amuck*, a Daffy Duck cartoon made in 1951 and released in 1953. Daffy Duck is persecuted by a cruel off-screen cartoonist who relentlessly alters Daffy's voice, location, clothing, appearance, and even his form. In the last frames of the short, the animator turns out to be Bugs Bunny. Bugs Bunny briefly stands in for both the animator and the audience, and he very lightly pokes fun at the notion of suspension of disbelief, without in any way destroying it.

Fiction vs. movies. This is from an interview Gary Lutz did for the *Believer*:

I think that movies are the ideal medium for getting characters from one place to another without making a big deal out of routine movement, and at the same time you can get the colors of the rooms or the neighborhoods, the weather, and emotionally convenient music on the soundtrack. Nobody has to come out with dulling declarations of "Then she got into the car" or "There he goes to the bathroom again." How-to books on the short story instruct writers to block out scenes as plays in miniature. Something in me wants to counter: Then why not just write a play or movie script instead? Why not try to do in a sentence or paragraph what can't be done in a shot or filmic sequence? Anyway, I am not one for plots—I think I recall somebody having remarked that the word "plot" itself gives off a whiff of burial dirt—and I find the concept of "cause and effect" to be tediously overrated.

I agree with this, although I also like to find interesting ways of describing how she got into the car, ways that no one else has done before, because whatever she was feeling as she got into her car was unique and perfectly suited for the moment she got into the car.

Writers vs. visual artists. An old friend of mine, Amanda Rea, kept a blog from her residency at the Fine Arts Work Center in Provincetown, from October 2007 to May 2008. At the beginning of her time there, she commented on the difference between the

visual artists and the writers—there are ten of each at the Work
Center (where I was also a fellow in 1984 and 1991). Here is the
heart of her remarks:

> Last night, there was a show-and-tell, in which the writers
> read and the artists showed slides of their work. Most of all,
> I enjoyed listening to the artists describe their work. They
> are unapologetic about their obsessions, and unquestioning.
> "I'm interested in furniture." "I'm interested in props." "I'm
> interested in machines that either work or work metaphori-
> cally." "I'm interested in myth-making." "I'm interested in
> making a life-sized colossal squid."

I envied the visual artists in Provincetown all the busywork
they had to do to get ready to paint or make sculpture. But I
also learned a great deal from them—from their reading and
their processes. It was easier (and more often fun) to watch a
painter make a painting (and work through drafts of it) than it
was to watch a writer make a story or poem. For one thing, I
was a writer, too, and there was a reflexive envy or comparison
that interfered with clear viewing of the process of other writers. I could see how a visual artist's creative mind worked, and
the points of contact between the two activities surprised me.
I was also occasionally devastated when a painting I'd grown
to love over several weeks was scraped down to canvas in a
fit of frustration. Painters, I saw, could not keep earlier drafts
of their work.

HOW TO USE THIS BOOK

The control panel. In *The 3 A.M. Epiphany*, I said each section of exercises should open a control panel of yet another literary concept, picking out for writers the little gears that control a single unparsed motion. Use these exercises to understand the small and large processes of writing fiction, memoir, and nonfiction. Combine two or three exercises together.

This bears repeating from *The 3 A.M. Epiphany*: "The individual exercises in this book might sometimes feel like isolated problems, remote from the larger overlapping issues of a story or a novel. By combining them, or by putting together stray elements from several different exercises in one piece, my students have achieved wonderful results."

For instance, you could put together the two exercises Parataxis (1) and Autism (79), which naturally belong together anyway (an autistic person often speaks in blunt, simple sentences without any connector phrases). The exercises are my ideas. Take them over and claim them as your own. Nobody will know. For the first exercise in the book, Parataxis, I say, "This fragment of fiction should concern a grown woman begging her mother not to remarry her father or a series of phone messages a nineteen-year-old man leaves for the woman who has just broken his heart." These two alternative plot prompts are simple and very different from each other. When I give story or plot ideas like this, they are less important than the structural or conceptual instructions for the exercises. Do not feel as committed to these parts of the exercises. Follow

your own instincts or your own better ideas for the plot. Or follow
the story line of something you're already working on.

Word limits. In this book, I suggest four word-length restrictions
for the exercises—250, 500, 750, or 1,000 words (which translates to roughly one, two, three, or four pages). I suggest these
lengths to match each exercise's inherent properties. The most
difficult exercises often have 250-word limits. The rare 1,000-
word exercises indicate a relative open-endedness of scope (although they are not license to blather). The majority of these
exercises have a 500-word limit. George Bernard Shaw occasionally apologized to his correspondents for not having had
time to write a *shorter* letter. The implication is that Shaw spent
time revising some letters and presumably reducing them. My
older brother Geoffrey often rewrote his letters to our grandparents when he was in his early teens. I was intimidated by this
activity and a bit scornful of the idea that one could rewrite a
loving letter to such wonderful people. I thought it robbed the
letter of spontaneity, a crucial part of the process of expressing
love to someone. I was wrong. Restricting the length of fiction
pushes you to come up with small gems rather than an unread-
able mass of material to sift through. The ability to compress
what you need to write into very small molds is one of the most
important things you can learn as a writer. I urge you to do whatever you can to obey these limits. At the same time, you can
and should think of these exercises as something much larger,
rangier, or baggier. But if an exercise grows into something

larger—a story, a novel idea—keep in mind the basic notion of restraint as you move along. I object to flabby, meandering fiction. Stick to the story or the concept. Make each sentence you write do one or two distinct and interesting things. Let each paragraph be an island of thought and similar activity.

Catalog and cross-reference. So you write ten of these exercises, and one turns out to be a very good idea. That's great. What about the other nine? Put them away, but don't forget them. You may find very good ideas for other fiction among these fragments one month or one year later. Train yourself to think of all your writing as useful, attachable, and interlocking, like LEGO pieces. I tell my graduate students to consider their teaching and their writing (when they've gone on to become a professor somewhere else) as interchangeable. Each is a form of writing. All the notes I take for my classes, all the variations on syllabi, all the paper assignments I dream up become useful—or are potentially useful—some time in the future, as parts of a book, an essay, a talk, or fiction. Writers should think of their lives as being made up of a lot of little writings. The key is to label every small thing you write so you can recover it later. Catalog, cross-reference, keep handwritten journals, save your e-mails in a separate file on your computer, type up intriguing pieces from your journals. Cannibalize all of your own writing. Most important of all, reread all your writing. It won't be useful if you've forgotten it and left it to languish in a basement file cabinet.

Get lost. K.C. Cole, a science writer and columnist for the *Los Angeles Times*, writing about science journalism in the *Columbia Journalism Review*, says, "In science, feeling confused is essential to progress. An unwillingness to feel lost, in fact, can stop creativity dead in its tracks ... [Science] editors, however, seem to absorb difficulty differently. If they don't understand something, they often think it can't be right—or that it's not worth writing about." I contend that confusion—or not knowing—is good for writing. Most writing teachers use exercises to stimulate students and help them find material. Writers rarely see the need for this process once they've started writing. But fiction exercises can be used at any time in the process—when you're stuck, confused, desperate, or even when you're working happily and fluently.

Stacy Schiff, in the *New York Times*, said, "Tea is said to have fueled the industrial revolution; caffeine has been credited with modern physics and chemistry. 'A mathematician,' the prolific, nonsleeping Paul Erdös liked to say, 'is a machine for turning coffee into theorems.'" Fiction exercises can be your coffee—energizers, clarifiers, simplifiers.

Using procrastination to your benefit. If you're facing a deadline you absolutely have to meet—for example, to write a paper for a class that meets in two hours, or a letter of recommendation, or a memo describing how the Y-screws cannot possibly fit into the X-holes your subsidiary in Indonesia has just manufactured ten thousand lots of—spend the first ten minutes of this precious time writing a piece of fiction, quickly, no editor over the shoulder, no stopping the fingers from their dance on the computer.

Use your own natural skills as a procrastinator for the good of your fiction (in this case at least). Find moments to write fiction when it is least convenient and most desirable to do so. You'll find, during these frantic little interludes of writing, that you often write beautifully, much better than when you give yourself an hour or four hours to do nothing but write beautifully. Why is this? We need constraints. We need to be ordered not to do something to want to do exactly that thing. The tension that creates good writing is often torqued by the constraints we feel while we're writing. The exercises in this book are tools for avoiding postponing writing (or overcoming writer's block), but there are times when procrastination is a good thing.

Stop thinking. In the *Boston Globe*, Gareth Cook talks about methods of decision-making that could easily be applied to the creative process:

> Scientists have some remarkable new advice for anyone who is struggling to make a difficult decision: Stop thinking about it. In a series of studies with shoppers and students, researchers found that people who face a decision with many considerations, such as what house to buy, often do not choose wisely if they spend a lot of time consciously weighing the pros and cons. Instead, the scientists conclude, the best strategy is to gather all of the relevant information—such as the price, the

number of bathrooms, the age of the roof—and then put the decision out of mind for a while.

Then, when the time comes to decide, go with what feels right. "It is much better to follow your gut," said Ap Dijksterhuis, a professor of psychology at the University of Amsterdam, who led the research. For relatively simple decisions, he said, it is better to use the rational approach. But the conscious mind can consider only a few facts at a time. And so with complex decisions, he said, the unconscious appears to do a better job of weighing the factors and arriving at a sound conclusion.

Read the instructions for whichever exercise you decide to do—read carefully. Apply the problems of the exercise to whatever you're planning to write about. If you are in the middle of a story or a novel, consider where the exercise would fit best and read around that area. But when you begin to write the actual exercise, stop thinking. Operate within the restraints of the exercise but don't think. Train your instincts. Let yourself swoon completely into the process.

Language is metaphor. Peter Calami reviewed Steven Pinker's book *The Stuff of Thought: Language as a Window Into Human Nature* in the *Toronto Star*, and he tried to tease out Pinker's essential argument about metaphor:

> "Rather than occasionally reaching for a metaphor to communicate, to a very large extent communication is the use of

metaphor," [Steven Pinker] says. "It could be that 95 percent of our speech is metaphorical, if you go back far enough in language." Why? Here, the teacher part of researcher and author Steven Pinker comes to the fore, offering a boring explanation and an interesting explanation, both with an element of truth. The boring explanation is that using metaphor is a quick-and-dirty way of expressing a new idea without the trouble of coining [notice the metaphor] and propagating a new word. "But that presupposes that the mind itself works metaphorically, that we see the abstract commonality between argument and war, between progress and motion. And it presupposes that the mind, at some level, must reason very concretely in order that these metaphors be understood and become contagious."

When I lived in Greece in 1988, I could read, with my rudimentary ancient Greek (one semester in college), the one common word on passing trucks, which was *metaphorai*—vehicles that transport material from one place to another. The exercises in this book are also metaphors. They help writers put together into a fragment of fiction two (or more) parts that don't go together—or wouldn't seem to go together at first glance. Let yourself be transported out of your fiction and into other fictions. Don't be afraid to work with the building blocks of fiction at all times.

The big picture. At the end of *The 3 A.M. Epiphany*, there is a little section called Limbing Up in which I said:

[W]riters ... need to teach themselves to write useful and necessary fiction, as well as good and competent fiction. Seek the higher ground, search for the material that challenges and changes you as a writer. These exercises should allow you to play with language on a small scale and build units of subject that help engineer the larger projects you want to do. Be ambitious, take on complex intellectual, political, and philosophical problems.

This is very important. The exercises in this book and in *The 3 A.M. Epiphany* might seem designed to make you concentrate only on small details. But keep the big picture in mind. Don't let the work you do on these exercises distract you from tackling moral problems, philosophical issues, and important subjects in your fiction. Exercises are not the goal. They should be the means of writing larger projects on significant questions. Behind the theory of these exercises is the simple idea that you should ask questions of the world. Ask your grandparents, parents, aunts and uncles, friends, and strangers why they do the things they do, what their essential philosophies are, and why they like what they like. Constantly ask yourself why you like what you like, too.

Writers ask questions. The best stories and novels are full of more questions than answers.

THE
EXERCISES

STYLE

Style is the words and the order of those words you choose to tell a story. In *The 3 A.M. Epiphany*, I quoted M.H. Abrams on the subject: Style "has traditionally been defined as the manner of linguistic expression in prose or verse—as *how* speakers or writers say whatever it is they say." The first exercises in *The 3 A.M. Epiphany* were about point of view. I begin *The 4 A.M. Breakthrough* with style because it is the molecular level of fiction.

PARATAXIS. Write a fragment of narrative in paratactic style. The best known example of parataxis is Julius Caesar's line to the Senate after a battle in what is now Turkey, recorded by Plutarch as, "I came, I saw, I conquered." This fragment of fiction should concern a grown woman begging her mother not to remarry her father or a series of phone messages a nineteen-year-old man leaves for the woman who has just broken his heart. (Look at the section The Control Panel at the beginning of this book [in What You Need to Know] for advice about how to take these story prompts.)

As you write this piece, keep in mind the image of the sentences as isolated islands of themselves, distant from the other sentence islands but within sight of each other. 500 words.

AT ITS SIMPLEST GRAMMATICAL LEVEL, according to the *Oxford English Dictionary*, parataxis is the placing of clauses one after another without showing how they connect (by coordination or subordination), as in *Tell me, how are you?* In *A Glossary of Literary Terms*, M.H. Abrams describes how this style works in fiction:

> Ernest Hemingway's style is characteristically paratactic. The members of this sentence from his novel *The Sun Also Rises* are joined merely by *ands*: "it was dim and dark and the pillars went high up, and there were people praying, and it smelt of incense, and there were some wonderful big buildings." The curt paratactic sentences in his short story "Indian Camp" omit all connectives: "The sun was coming over the hills. A bass jumped, making a circle in the water. Nick trailed his hand in the water. It felt warm in the sharp chill of the morning."

One explanation for this method, which Hemingway and Gertrude Stein pioneered, is that writers began to distrust the whole structure of cause and effect in narrative. Life, they might have been theorizing, was far more complicated and yet less connected. Experience and consciousness are scatterings of details that could mean something when joined together, but the meaning is subjective, not scientific. The short story writer and translator Lydia Davis noticed that fiction in the twentieth century has steadily moved away from hypotaxis (with its many subordinate clauses and phrases) toward parataxis in the patterning of its sentences. In my own fiction, I use hypotaxis in my rough drafts (employing *although* and *because* promiscuously) and parataxis in my later drafts.

Here is a nice example of hypotaxis, from E.B. White's essay "The Ring of Time": "After the lions had returned to their cages, creeping angrily through the chutes, a little bunch of us drifted away and into an open doorway nearby, where we stood for a while in semi-darkness watching a big brown circus horse go harumphing around the practice ring."

2

PARAGRAPHS AS CONTAINERS. Write five paragraphs of narrative about one individual who has decided to stop spending so much time with a gang of friends. Each paragraph should be about an isolated problem of this larger issue. All five paragraphs should have overlapping characters, but you do not have to follow one character all the way through the five paragraphs. Think of the paragraphs as tiny stories in and of themselves. Separate each paragraph by a space. 1,000 words.

THIS IS A QUESTION OF STORY VS. STORAGE. *Paragraph* is defined by the *Oxford English Dictionary* as: "A distinct passage or section of a text, usually composed of several sentences, dealing with a particular point, a short episode in a narrative, a single piece of direct speech, etc." Even the *Oxford English Dictionary* has to trail off in its description of the word with "etc." Paragraphs are boxes into which we put information. Some fiction writers excel at sentences (Samuel Beckett) and some at paragraphs (Isak Dinesen). What I hope you discover when you do this exercise is that you can move your narrative along much more efficiently and interestingly if you snip the connective tissue between your paragraphs. Let each new paragraph in your writing signal another set of thoughts and ideas.

3

ETYMOLOGIES. Take four words that seem to recur in your fiction. Study their etymological histories. How will you find these four words that recur in your fiction? If you have all or even some of your fiction in digital format, click on Edit in the main toolbar (of Microsoft Word). Then click on the Find... option. You'll simultaneously have to reread your old fiction and see if you come across repeated words.

The words you choose should be meaty and complex, preferably with a long etymological history. Use the older meanings (without the word) as well as modern synonyms. Collect some sentences with these etymologies rewritten into relatively normal-sounding narrative sentences. Eventually, you will have a piece of prose that is something of a comment on your previous stories (or novels). 500 words.

ROBERT FULFORD, in the *National Post*, examines the history of one word:

> The evolution of the word *cunning* suggests that a history could be written through changing word-meanings. In the fourteenth century, *cunning* meant erudition, and in the sixteenth Sir Thomas More described virtues such as "chastity, liberality, temperance, cunning." But perhaps English speakers noticed that wisdom could be put to corrupt ends. They shifted the adjective from the Positive column to the Negative.
>
> By the eighteenth century it clearly meant knavery. The sentimental nineteenth century added a new meaning—appealing, sweet. Dickens in *Martin Chuzzlewit* tells us of tea served with "cunning teacakes." By 1887, it described a child who was "piquantly interesting." Today, a more blatant use emerges: A British ad agency called Cunning promises "guerrilla marketing," boasting British Airways and Levi's as clients.

_____ (4) _____

LANGUAGE IS ALWAYS AN ABBREVIATION. Take these five words, "Language is always an abbreviation." Replace each word with the next closest (and most interesting) word in an imaginary dictionary. Don't use an actual dictionary. Try to think of a word that would follow each word in this group. You do not need to find a word of equal length, nor of the same sort (a verb, noun, etc.). Once you've selected your replacement words (adding an *s* or an *ed*), manipulate the words a bit so the sentence makes some sense. Next, find five new words from these replacement words, using only the letters of each new replacement word (make a sort of anagram from the five new words). You do not need to use all of the letters of each word and you can use any letter more than once. Once you've finished selecting a new set of five words, again manipulate the words slightly to make "sense" of the new sentence (adding a letter or two that doesn't exist in the original). You will have three five-word sentences now. These will be the titles of three paragraphs. Write the paragraphs with these five-word sentences in mind. What I hope happens to you when you attempt this exercise is you see and feel the opposite of the idea that language is always an abbreviation. 250 words.

I GATHERED THIS short sentence from John Berger's essay "Post-Scriptum," in a retrospective book about the painter Cy Twombly's career, *Audible Silence*:

> A writer continually struggles for clarity *against* the language he's using, or, more accurately, against the common usage of that language. He doesn't see language with the readability and clarity of something print- ed out. He sees it, rather, as a terrain full of illegibilities, hidden paths,

impasses, surprises, and obscurities. Its map is not a dictionary but the whole of literature and perhaps everything ever said. Its obscurities, its lost senses, its self-effacements come about for many reasons—because of the way words modify each other, write themselves over each other, cancel one another out, because the unsaid always counts for as much, or more, than the said, and because language can never recover what it signifies. Language is always an abbreviation.

5

THE LETTER A. Write a story about an ox or a cow. Make the title of the piece one word, which begins with the letter A. Then choose 20 words that begin with the letter A. Let those 20 words stand alone for a while. Then slowly write a sentence or two or three around each word. Let these groups of sentences stand for a while (as you would a cake or a baked chicken). After a good while, see if you can find an order to the sentences you've made. You can split up the sentences that originally belonged to a word. Remember, in this story, an ox or a cow plays a significant role. 500 words.

ALLAN HALEY, in Fonts.com, says:

> Some say the Phoenicians chose the head of an ox to represent the "A" sound (for the Phoenicians, this was actually a glottal stop). The ox was a common, important animal to the Phoenicians. It was their main power source for heavy work. Oxen plowed the fields, harvested crops, and hauled food to market. Some sources also claim that the ox was often the main course at meals. A symbol for the ox would have been an important communication tool for the

Phoenicians. It somewhat naturally follows that an ox symbol would be the first letter of the alphabet.

6

THE LETTER B. Write about shelter this time, with the same rules as in The Letter A (exercise 5). 750 words.

MORE ALLAN HALEY:

> Many people consider shelter to be the second most important ingredient for human survival. Coincidentally, the second letter in our alphabet evolved from the ancient Egyptian hieroglyph signifying shelter. Although the designs are somewhat different, there is a recognizable correlation between this Egyptian hieroglyph and the second letter of the Phoenician alphabet. The Phoenicians called this letter *beth*, their word for "house." The name was eventually carried over into names and places in the Bible, including Bethel (house of God) and Bethlehem (house of bread).

René Etiemble also notes, "Although human beings have been living and dying for a million years, they have been writing for only six thousand years."

7

POTHOLES. Take 750 words of one of your own old failed stories—only 750 words. The first goal of this exercise is to train you to choose the most successful part of an unsuccessful story. Or maybe the first goal is to teach you to figure out which are your failed stories and why. When you've given up on a story and don't have anything to lose, start taking chances, making bold moves you wouldn't otherwise attempt. Next, eliminate two of every three sentences throughout the fragment (leaving one sentence standing); it doesn't matter which two you choose. You do not need to cut the second of three sentences each time, for example. What's left will likely be difficult to understand. But you may feel a pattern of sense nevertheless pulses (narrative threads often remain even after great damage to the narrative).

Now, you can add sentences or phrases; however, you can't rearrange the original order of your cut-up story. Finally, try to keep the feeling of sentences and even paragraphs missing between all the sentences of the final draft. These missing sentences and paragraphs don't need to be obvious, but they should be tangible. Efficient storytelling is all about leaving out unnecessary steps. The final product should be 500 words.

"THE WEDDING WAS CURT and almost entirely without result. At no point during the ceremony did the minister let anybody but himself be the center of attention. The halfway decent thing about the reception was that the tables were so narrow, the guests could sit on only one side." This is 60 percent of Gary Lutz's tiny story "Being Good in October," from his collection *Stories in the Worst Way*. What has happened between these sentences? Between the first and second sentences, there is a tenuous connection—the egotistical minister. Or is the minister simply doing what ministers do—*preside* over a wedding? Between the second and third sentences, the focus shifts away from the minister and the wedding to the guests (and the most important guest of all, the unseen narrator of these events, who never really reveals herself).

Why is it useful for writers to test their readers' skills at making illogical leaps from sentence to sentence or paragraph to paragraph? What usually happens between sentences or ellipses or chapters in stories? Writers should train themselves to leave out as much as they put into a story and to manipulate (in a sense) what they leave out—letting the absent material poke the story in the side so readers get a greater sense of the story below the story, rather than the surface narrative. Life is full of stuff below the surface of reality—it's often called The Past. Narrative ought to have a pretty surface, but it can also be like a frozen pond you're walking along with your high school boyfriend—all squeezes, sighs, and meaningful glances until you come across your boyfriend's identical twin brother below the ice staring up at you, arms spread out imploringly, the word *C-c-cold* clearly frozen on his dead lips. Meaning is often created by the logical gaps in our fiction. In my own fiction I fight the urge to construct smooth and flowing narrations because I think smoothness is a vanity, a distortion of the story's reality. All writers think they're realists (no matter their literary political leanings), but writers may understand from this exercise that meaning is also produced offstage, by the light technicians, the costume people, the guy who operates the trap door and elevators out of sight of the audience.

Think of why you make great leaps from sentence to sentence or paragraph to paragraph—are they always useful and emotionally interesting, or are they sometimes ways of avoiding saying what you want to say directly? Go deeper—risk embarrassment, silliness, and sadness.

---- 8)--------

RHETORICAL QUESTIONS. Write a fragment of story using mostly rhetorical questions. You can write a plain, vanilla sentence that is not a rhetorical question every five sentences, though you don't have to be strict about this. You could do it every six sentences sometimes. 500 words.

WHY WOULD ONE WANT to write in rhetorical questions (which itself is a rhetorical question)? Why not? A rhetorical question is asked only for effect, and it expects no answer. Like another exercise in *The 3 A.M. Epiphany*, Imperatives, which asks writers to use only commands or imperative statements, this one is going to show you both how hard it is to make narrative out of this sort of restriction and how easily the narrative seems to flow out around the edges of the very restrictions that make narratizing so difficult.

---- 9)--------

ESSAY FICTION. Write a piece of fiction that sounds, most of the time, like an essay, but periodically degrades (or improves) into fictional narrative. The essay should be about something specific that matters a great deal to you—cats, flavored coffee, people who say "foward" instead of "forward." According to M.H. Abrams, the essay is "any short composition in prose that undertakes to discuss a matter, express a point of view, persuade us to accept a thesis on any subject." Abrams distinguishes the essay from the dissertation by its "lack of pretension to be a systematic or complete exposition." So the essay is the perfect counterpart to the short story—a loose collection of ideas held together by the say-so of the voice telling us the story or essay. This is an experiment in voice and authority. The essayist is at least to a certain degree an authority. The narrator of a short story can be convincing or he can be a liar. 500 words.

LAURA MILLER reviewed Don DeLillo's 9/11 novel in *Salon*:

> The weaknesses of *Falling Man* are DeLillo's long-standing ones. Most of them spring from the fact that he is an essayist at heart, who presumably chose the novel because it is the most exalted and revered literary form of our time—and DeLillo is not the sort of writer willing to risk being insufficiently exalted and revered. The characters in *Falling Man* are typically sketchy and the dialogue improbable; everyone speaks in exactly the same stagy, portentous manner as the mouthpiece characters in an experimental play. (What woman, being deserted by a lover, would say, "Do I know how to make one thing out of another, without pretending? Can I stay who I am, or do I have to become all those other people who watch someone walk out the door? We're not other people, are we?")

I like Laura Miller's criticism generally, but this is a ridiculous statement ("What woman, being deserted by a lover, would say ..."). This imagines that there is some kind of exact reality that is repeated over and over again, which we must all, as writers and as human beings, conform to. Another interesting but deeply flawed critique of DeLillo is that he is an essayist at heart and not really a novelist. There is no such thing as the "novel." Or it has always been a hybrid thing, a collection of genres and styles and appropriations. What is wonderful about DeLillo is that he puts philosophy in the mouths of his ordinary characters, that he lets them speak for him (presumably), or that he lets them speak from deep within themselves, saying the ideal things they shouldn't ordinarily be able to articulate. The American minimalists believed powerfully in the essential inarticulateness of Americans, especially in the working class. DeLillo is not a realist, and Laura Miller makes the mistake of imagining he is because he can be so faithful to certain kinds of reality.

USED LITERATURE

Rewriting, revisiting, and reinventing other people's works of art is an old and noble activity. Poets, painters, composers, and novelists have done it from the beginning of these art forms. Until the Renaissance, it was actually improper and sinful to create something new without any reference to the previous work that was being remade. Great art is often at the very least a conscious response to other great art. Tolstoy wrote *Anna Karenina* in reaction to Flaubert's *Madame Bovary* (almost a hostile takeover). This section of exercises works specifically with the idea of renovation and response.

10

SORROW-ACRE. Take a story you love (as I love Isak Dinesen's "Sorrow-Acre"). Write three different summaries of the story, in 200 words, in 50 words, and in 10 words. Let these three summaries sit on your computer or in your desk drawer for a month (mark your calendar or set up some type of electronic reminder so you'll know when to go back to the summaries). Now add narrative prose of some kind—perhaps imitating the tone of the summaries—between these short pieces of prose. Connect them to each other, even though they are all paragraphs or sentences about the same story. Once you've added these connections, go over the whole thing and slowly turn it into a coherent story. 750 words.

IN SUMMARIES YOU CAN AND SHOULD rearrange the chronology of the story or novel. Arrange in order of importance, not in order of occurrence. Ask yourself simple questions to provoke a proper and effective summary: What happens? How does it happen? Why does it happen? Who are the key players? What do they, or we, learn from the actions of the story? Above all, a summary should be concise and to the point. It is not a para-phrase of the story, a retelling of the story in your own words. It should be the boiled-down essence of the story. In order to summarize, in a way, you have to have an opinion of the story, but the summary should also be a relatively objective reading of the story. Summary is the best tool you have in your criticism of other people's writing, and in the end it can be-come the tool you use most successfully in your own writing. A summary tells you what your writing is doing. You need to know what your writing does in other readers' eyes in order to be a successful writer.

Here are three of my own summaries of "Sorrow-Acre." In 198 words:

The story appears to be set some time before 1800. A woman is given a chance to save her son from jail. The lord of the manor, who has the power of life and death on his land, does not have enough evidence to convict her son of the crime, so he tells her she can win her son's freedom by sowing an entire acre of his land in one day.

The lord's nephew, recently returned from abroad with new ideas foreign to his homeland, disagrees with his uncle over this punishment. Their disagreement is cast in terms of Greek and Norse mythologies. The nephew finds the Norse gods more inspiring. The uncle feels it was easier for the Norse gods to be good because they were not all-powerful. He says to his nephew that because of the Greek gods' "omnipotence they take over the woe of the universe." The lord is complaining here of the burdens of his own power. The manor represents an Eden. It is no coincidence that the nephew's name is Adam and the uncle is known only as "the old lord." The mother sows the acre, frees her son, and dies from exhaustion.

In 53 words:

A grim fairy tale about how land gives authority over life and death. A lord owns the land, which gives him the right to weigh life and death. The land, in the end, carries out the punishment. The lord's nephew, who opposes his uncle's notion of justice, is driven out of this Eden.

And in 12 words:

Adam leaves Eden because he disagrees with his lord's idea of justice.

YOUR SWANN. Write a letter from one of your fictional characters to another. In this letter, tell a brief history of another (third) character over many years who plays at least three significantly different roles over the letter writer's lifetime. The person receiving this letter may know a little bit about your character's acquaintance, but she shouldn't know too much. Because you'll have so little space to expand upon this character, it's okay to use narrative shorthand, as all letters do. 500 words.

MARCEL PROUST describes the important character Swann in *In Search of Lost Time* (earlier called *Remembrance of Things Past*):

> ...[T]he Swann who was a familiar figure in all the clubs of those days differed hugely from the Swann created by my great-aunt when, of an evening, in our little garden at Combray, after the two shy peals had sounded from the gate, she would inject and vitalize with everything she knew about the Swann family the obscure and shadowy figure who emerged, with my grandmother in his wake, from the dark background and who was identified by his voice. But then, even in the most insignificant details of our daily life, none of us can be said to constitute a material whole, which is identical for everyone and need only be turned up like a page in an account-book or the record of a will; our social personality is a creation of the thoughts of other people.

Swann is the first "character" is Proust's *In Search of Lost Time*. He is the first stranger outside the narrator's immediate family who impinges on his childhood. He appears as someone who takes his mother away from putting young Marcel to bed. Then he is the father of Marcel's first crush, Gilberte. Later, when Marcel is an adult, Swann becomes his friend and mentor. Swann represents, for both Marcel the character in the book and for Marcel Proust the author of the book, the ideal of a rounded character, not just with many moving parts at any one moment in the book, but rounded by layers of different personas through time. We all know many people over different epochs of our own (and their) lives. Our parents, for instance, are impossibly important and dominating when we are children, annoying and intrusive when we are teenagers, maybe friends in our twenties (though they may still treat us like thirteen-year-olds), and finally they become our own children in their declining years.

12

THE SYSTEMS NOVEL. Write a very short systems story. By definition, this is impossible. A systems novel takes on a huge system and pretends to (or occasionally actually does) explain the system. So a systems short story would have to dramatically condense the information that usually mounts up endlessly in such books as Thomas Pynchon's *Gravity's Rainbow* or David Foster Wallace's *Infinite Jest*. Your story should attempt to describe both a system and a couple of human beings involved in (or trying to break free from) this system. For example, a recent college graduate is writing for an early morning news show at a local medium-sized city TV station. He rises at two each morning, gets to the station by 3:30, and begins his research for the day's news stories, which have to be ready for broadcast and teleprompter at five. He is both proud of himself for this first job out of college and deeply depressed by the hours, the overbearing control of the producers, and the inanity of the talent (the newscasters). He is also participating in an obvious form of censorship of events going on in the world, pitching the stories to the producers' ideas of what the audience can understand and bear. What is frustrating and fascinating to this news writer is that he *likes* censoring the news his audience will receive. He is both a cynic and a happy participant in the activity he is cynical about. You have only 500 words to make this work—a ridiculously small frame to pour out such a large topic. But that's the point of this exercise.

TOM LECLAIR COINED THE PHRASE in his book *In the Loop: Don DeLillo and the Systems Novel*. Here's how LeClair sees the inner workings of *White Noise*: DeLillo's characters "try to understand new information rather than cause events to happen; they learn the processes in which they participate, rather than dictate circumstances." Borrowed from the sciences, systems theory is a paradigm one can use to analyze or characterize any group of things that work together to produce a cohesive result. Systems novels and paranoia are common bedfellows. Look at how Pynchon and DeLillo examine CIA officers, military personnel, and radio disk jockeys through the prism of paranoid democracy. This last phrase actually applies to computers. According to Philip Elmer-Dewitt in *TIME*, "Fault-tolerant computers like those built by Stratus, Tandem, and, for that matter, AT&T reduce runaway system errors by a kind of 'paranoid democracy,' where modules working in parallel constantly evaluate whether their electronic co-workers are 'sane' or 'crazy.'" Occasionally paranoia is a good thing.

The old idea of epic poetry was the portrayal of life by values. The novel added to this equation the novel's portrayal of life by time. Time was abstract before the novel. After the novel, we have a sense of the personal identity subsisting through duration and yet being changed by the flow of experience. The novel contains time, as no other art form does. So you've got your work cut out for you here.

────────────── 13)──────────────

BIG TWO-HEARTED RIVER. Write another version of this great story originally published in the collection *In Our Time*. Ernest Hemingway's two-part story is about a man who has just returned from World War I, and he's shell-shocked. Hemingway never tells us these two facts. He simply sends the character out into the northern peninsula of Michigan to fish and camp, alone the whole time. The character does not interact with anyone after the first few pages of the story. The landscape is both beautiful and scarred—there has been a recent forest fire over the whole area where Nick Adams fishes and camps.

Be faithful to the Hemingway original, but you will clearly want to make this story your own. Read the story several times. Think about the way Nick contemplates the natural world and the human interferences with it. Feel free to change the activity, from fishing to mountain biking, for example, and the "untold circumstance" of the character from shell-shock to abuse or divorce. Because of the word limit on this exercise, you'll only be able to rewrite a fragment of the original story. 750 words.

────────────── 14)──────────────

A CANTICLE FOR LEIBOWITZ. Write about a shopping list, as if this shopping list had much more meaning than it could possibly hold. Imagine this shopping list found hundreds of years later and analyzed for hidden meaning (or perhaps without any understanding of its original and simple meanings). You might want to stay in the present (as opposed to science fiction): a wife's shopping list found by the husband she has just left; or a to-do list found after a child has run away. 500 words.

WALTER MILLER'S *A Canticle for Leibowitz* was published in 1960. It is the story of humankind hundreds of years after nuclear war. The book is set in the southwestern desert of the former United States, in a monastery founded by Jewish engineer Isaac Leibowitz, who survived the war and converted to Catholicism. A small part of the book involves the illumination of "manuscripts" that survived Leibowitz himself, including a shopping list. The brothers in the monastery, centuries later, do not know what to make of this fragment of phrases: "pound pastrami, can kraut, six bagels—bring home for Emma," but they dutifully write and rewrite the shopping list, as monks in medieval Europe did for ancient Greek philosophy, trying to illuminate its meaning.

This exercise is a specialized version of an exercise from *The 3 A.M. Epiphany*, The List. The contemporary, accepted meaning of the word *list* is a catalog or roll consisting of a series of names, figures, or words. In early use, a list was a catalog of the names of persons engaged in the *same* duties or connected with the *same* object (useful to keep that in mind—a gathering of details around one concept). The word *list* derives from an old French word for a strip of paper. Obsolete uses of the word include art, craft, or cunning. Pleasure, job, and delight, as well as longing and appetite, precede the notion of inventory. One also lists, inclining to one side, as a ship or a drunk does. An *inventory* is a detailed list of items, such as goods and chattels, or parcels of land, found to have been in the possession of a person at his *decease* or *conviction*, sometimes with a statement of the nature and value of each. *Inventory* and *list* both represent a mortal accounting of the things left of a life. Novels have had similar urges, to account for the things and actions left behind by a life.

—————————————— 15)——————————————

IHAB HASSAN. Write an essay about one pair of these notions: semantics vs. rhetoric; distance vs. participation; design vs. chance; or purpose vs. play. See below for explanations of these terms. Let this essay slowly evolve into fiction. The person speaking the essay could begin to sound a little less sure of himself. At the beginning, the essay could follow the familiar patterns of essay writing—cool, objective language, good examples, efficient prose. You could let that method break down a bit. An example becomes odd or drifts off on a tangent. Don't let the essay style completely degrade. Keep us thinking we're reading an essay, rather than a story, as long as possible. 750 words.

IHAB HASSAN, IN HIS ESSAY "Toward a Concept of Postmodernism" (from his book *The Postmodern Turn: Essays in Postmodern Theory and Culture*), opposes a number of literary terms under the headings Modernism and Postmodernism. I'm not particularly interested in this artificial divide, but the binary oppositions are interesting by themselves as triggers for writing. Here are three of the oppositions: *semantics* (under modernism) and *rhetoric* (under postmodernism). Semantics is the study of meaning; rhetoric is the study of effective use of language. Another is *distance* (under modernism) and *participation* (under postmodernism). The author in a modernist work, according to Flaubert, is supposed to be like a god paring his nails, uninvolved in the process of the art, disinterested, offering no opinions. Presumably, the postmodern author and the reader participate together in the construction of the fictional world being spun out. A third pair is *design* and *chance* (or *purpose* and *play*). Postmodern fiction is supposed to prefer chance and playfulness, and the modernists loved the architecture of their novels so much that (sometimes) they were not terribly livable environments. Modernist architects were accused of a similar hostility to the people who actually had to live and work in their buildings. Donald Barthelme, the postmodernist fiction writer extraordinaire, grew up with a modernist architect for a father, whom he battled, literally and figuratively, all his working life.

16

BRUNO SCHULZ. Write a short story about your own family. Use only the words *Father*, *Mother*, *Sister*, *Brother* when appropriate, instead of names. Tell a story without appearing to tell a story. Use your family as if they were mythical universal figures, but be as honest and accurate as you can. Don't worry about any chronology or cause and effect. If it helps, tell yourself you won't show this story to anyone after you've written it. 1,000 words.

BRUNO SCHULZ USES a few key characters throughout his stories. They are not *built*, except perhaps for the character Father, but they *exist*. In Schulz we have a world in which Walt Disney meets Franz Kafka, whom Schulz translated into Polish. The father in the stories is frequently mad, a literary relative of Kafka's more frightening father. He speaks in a cracked, almost sensible philosophy of wooden mannequins, like the following from "Treatise on Tailors' Dummies":

> "Who knows," [Father] said, "how many suffering, crippled, fragmentary forms of life there are, such as the artificially created life of

chests and tables quickly nailed together, crucified timbers, silent martyrs to cruel human inventiveness. The terrible transplantation of incompatible and hostile races of wood, their merging into one misbegotten personality."

Schulz is one of my favorite writers. I can't say how he's influenced me, but there is one accident of composition we share. Schulz's translator, Jerzy Ficowski, writes about who Schulz addressed his stories to, in his introduction to *The Street of Crocodiles*:

> Lacking the courage to address *readers*, he tried at first to write for *a* reader, a recipient of his letters. When at last, around 1930, he found a partner for this exchange in the person of Deborah Vogel, a poet and doctor of philosophy who lived in Lvov, his letters—even then often masterpieces of the epistolary art—underwent a metamorphosis, becoming daring fragments of dazzling prose. His correspondent, greatly excited, urged him to continue. It was in this way, letter by letter, piece by piece, that *The Street of Crocodiles* came into being, a literary work enclosed a few pages at a time in envelopes and dropped into the mailbox.

I've done this myself, in my postcard stories, sometimes consciously adding to whatever novel I've been working on, sometimes not. One aspect of Schulz's method I wonder about. Did he keep copies of the letters he'd sent? If he didn't, this form of composition is all the more impressive and terrifying. Relying on a correspondent to take care of your growing stories—and not throw them away or not care about them—that's both brave and foolish.

---(17)---

ISAAC BABEL. Write a narrative about a brilliant skinny journalist with glasses who is embedded with soldiers in a desperate and dangerous set of battles in an awful, unwinnable war. This can be any war you want—recent or distant, real or imagined. 750 words.

IN HIS STORY "The Death of Dolgushov," Babel captures with poetic simplicity the effect of machine-gun fire: "Bullets began to whine and wail, their lament growing unbearably. Bullets struck the earth and fumbled in it, quivering with impatience." The story follows a narrator (a stand-in for Babel himself) who is faced with the agonizing responsibility of killing his severely wounded friend Dolgushov, who does not want to be tortured by the advancing Polish Army (he knows they can't take him with them in their retreat). Babel captures the madness of war in this simple decision his character makes—he won't shoot Dolgushov. The commander is disgusted by the narrator's cowardice, and he casually shoots his soldier. War is a reasonable response to insanity.

In a later story, "Guy de Maupassant," the young narrator works with a rich banker's wife, helping with her translation of his beloved Maupassant.

> I took the manuscript with me, and in Kazantsev's attic, among my sleeping friends, spent the night cutting my way through the tangled undergrowth of her prose. It was not such dull work as it might seem. A phrase is born into the world both good and bad at the same time. The secret lies in a slight, an almost invisible twist.

The lever should rest in your hand, getting warm, and you can only turn it once, not twice.

In both of these tiny examples of Babel's prose, you see the way he humanizes objects and activities that are not necessarily human—bullets "quivering with impatience" and the lever one holds when writing a translation from one language to another.

──────────────────── 18)────────────────────

NO TIME. Write a fragment of fiction in which there is no (apparent) passage of time, and there are only children and the very old. No passage of time could mean timeless, or it could mean that time seems to move very slowly (the way a Nicholson Baker novel does—a microscopic examination of reality). The second part of the instruction is simpler. Young children see time quite differently than grownups ("how long until we get to Uncle Bill's?" asked every fifteen minutes, when Uncle Bill's house is six hours away). The very old see time move more quickly, but they also have less to do with their time. 750 words.

LAURA MILLER IN the *New York Times* quoted Robert Penn Warren, noting that "there's no time in Hemingway, there are only moments in themselves, moments of action. There are no parents and no children," whereas "in Faulkner there are always the very old and the very young. Time spreads and is the important thing, the terrible thing." A reviewer for Amazon.com who calls himself or herself Sofomtext says this about a novel by Susan Choi: "She re-imagines and re-creates a palpable 'real' universe that stops time." Great art stops time.

---(**19**)---

GRACE PALEY. Buy Grace Paley's *Collected Stories*. Read "The Pale Pink Roast." Write a fictional reaction to this story. 500 words.

PALEY'S STORY "The Pale Pink Roast" shows us, in choppy action and conversation sequences, the relationship between a woman and her ex-husband (the father of her daughter). They meet in a park. The banter is funny, tart, expressing her frustration with him and his blithe disregard. A sort of camaraderie forms; the ex-husband finds a babysitter in the park to look after their daughter, and the two go back to her new apartment nearby. He does the kind of busywork that a husband would do, and they have sex. At the conclusion of their encounter, she reveals that she's remarried and is waiting for her husband to join her. Her ex is genuinely shocked and even perhaps hurt—or hurt on behalf of the new husband. But the woman says she did it for love. This is still shocking fifty years after it was written. Writer Vivian Gornick says, "Strictly speaking, women and men in Paley stories do not fall in love with each other, they fall in love with the desire to feel alive."

---(**20**)---

PALIMPSEST. Take ten sentences from the first paragraph of E.L. Doctorow's novel *Ragtime* and add a sentence between each sentence—an explanation, a connective tissue, a reason for going from one sentence to the next (which is not always clear in *Ragtime*). You'll be trying to short-circuit the associative prose of Doctorow.

Associative means the process of forming mental connections between sensations, ideas, or memories. Psychoanalysts ask patients to free-associate from a word ("bird" causing a patient to think of his mother's hawk-like nose and the habit she had of watching him sleep every night from his bedroom doorway, her hawk nose the only identifying characteristic in the dark). The opposite of this is cause and effect, which is how traditional narrative operates. After you've written these twenty sentences, write another fifteen sentences as epilogue. The epilogue should be casual commentary on the effect of interlarding sentences between sentences of another writer. The final product will not be an essay. Nor will it be fiction. 500 words.

WHAT I'M GETTING AT in this exercise is an understanding of how Doctorow's sentences work—he lists things, presenting a collage of objects and ideas from the past in an attempt to catalog the dizzying multiplicity of past details. Here are the first ten sentences (more or less) of *Ragtime*:

> Teddy Roosevelt was President. The population customarily gathered in great numbers either out of doors for parades, public concerts, fish fries, political picnics, social outings, or indoors in meeting halls, vaudeville theaters, operas, ballrooms. There seemed to be no entertainment that did not involve great swarms of people ... Women were stouter then. They visited the fleet carrying white parasols. Everyone wore white in summer. Tennis racquets were hefty and the racquet faces were elliptical. There was a lot of sexual fainting. There were no Negroes. There were no immigrants.

Notice, for instance, between the sentences about sexual fainting and Negroes the possible connection: women fainting at the mere sight of a Negro male.

_____ 21)_____

ROBERT CREELEY. Imagine overhearing a conversation between two intimates—a married couple, siblings, or old friends who have weathered many fights. Your observer has happened upon these two people in the middle of a heated, emotional conversation. The person who hears this talk cannot be seen. Work at both the intensity of the words and the inarticulateness a moment like this can provoke. 500 words.

ROBERT CREELEY'S POEM "I Know a Man" has been called *the* poem of the 1950s.

> As I sd to my
> friend, because I am
> always talking, -- John, I
>
> sd, which was not his
> name, the darkness sur-
> rounds us, what
>
> can we do against
> it, or else, shall we &
> why not, buy a goddamn big car,
>
> drive, he sd, for
> christ's sake, look
> out where yr going.

Stephen Burt, in an essay on the work of Robert Creeley in the *London Review of Books*, puts it this way about the great, laconic poet: "To listen to Creeley at his best is to listen, often uncomfortably, to men and women speaking behind closed doors, to hear what they say to themselves and to each other when they do not know what else to do." This is one of the hardest things to do as a writer—to say things that people do say, but only in the most uncensored moments of their lives. Observe Creeley's mixture of humor, self-criticism, honesty, and abruptness. Imitate that in your fragment of fiction.

22

POETRY & ENGLAND. Grab an anthology of great British poetry—one of the Norton anthologies, *The Columbia Anthology of British Poetry*, or a volume of *The Oxford Anthology of English Poetry*. Browse through the book. Seek out a handful of poems that you want to return to again and again. If you already have favorite poems, go back to them and handwrite them on free sheets of paper so you can feel the poem flowing through your fingers. Do this for five poems—poetry you've always liked or poetry you've just discovered. Take the best lines from these five poems and put them at the top of your virtual page (on your computer; or on your actual page if you still write by hand or typewriter). One of these lines in some form or another will be your title. Save this file, turn off the computer, and leave the writing alone for a few days.

When you go back to this page with five lines (or parts of lines) of great poetry, select the one that will be your title. Cut the other four lines and paste them onto another file or page. You'll go back to these lines in the next twenty minutes, from time to time, to rescue parts or all of these lines and insert them into your fragment of fiction. Set a timer or alarm clock for twenty minutes. Write without stopping, although you may also edit and cut material as you're going along. Write about a character who is trying to express a very difficult thought to someone else. Let this poetry guide you. When you're done, you should have about 500 words.

BRYAN APPLEYARD, in his essay "Poetry and the English Imagination," talks about the history of poetry in England:

> Poetry has no serious contenders as the English national art. Ah, it is often said, but Shakespeare wrote plays. And so he did. But consider these plays. *Hamlet* is a weird drama made magnificent by a torrent of peerless poetry, and I have always thought of it as a long poem whose cosmic structure seems to pivot on the words "We defy augury." Shakespeare is the greatest playwright on earth, but he is heaven's poet. And the list of his poet-compatriots—Chaucer, Browning, Dryden, Wordsworth, Clare, Donne, Auden, Tennyson, Keats, Pope, Herbert, etc. etc.—closes the case. We are a nation defined by and consisting of poets. To deny this is to deny England.
>
> Why this should be is open to infinite speculation. It is often said that Protestantism turned us away from the image to the word, but that was late in the day. Some talk of the landscape or the weather, but other nations have those. More significant may be the legacy of Roman occupation, which left the English with a unique sense of home as land, a poetic idea that runs through Clare and Wordsworth to Auden's "In Praise of Limestone." But the truth, I suspect, is that it is the English language itself which made us poets. This is, of course, unprovable, not least because of the chicken and egg question—did the language make the English poets or did the

English make the language poetic? But, if only subjectively, I think
some kind of case can be made.

Poetry has been a resource for my fiction from my beginnings as a writer.
Poets were my first writer friends. Poetry served as a tempting alternative for
me, although I never did it very well (from the age of seventeen I've always
called myself a fiction writer). Fiction writers should know poetry deeply,
steal from it, think in its terms, and play with its rules and methods. Reading
poetry demands a concentration fiction is not supposed to demand. The
great realist and modernist fiction writers of the nineteenth and twentieth
centuries—Flaubert, Stein, Joyce, Beckett, and Hemingway—approached
the process of fiction as poets once had, carefully looking for the right word
and only that word. Some later fiction writers have lamented this trend.

Here's an example of one of my own favorite poems, John Donne's
"Elegy: To his Mistress Going to Bed" (the second stanza):

> License my roving hands, and let them go
> Behind, before, above, between, below.
> Oh my America, my new found land,
> My kingdom, safeliest when with one man man'd,
> My mine of precious stones, my Empiree,
> How blest am I in this discovering thee.
> To enter in these bonds is to be free,
> Then where my hand is set my seal shall be.

Later in his life Donne (1572–1631) was Dean of St. Paul's, a significant
position in the Anglican Church, but in his youth he wrote some of the
sexiest poems in the language. The excerpt above might seem to be about
something else—exploring the world and discovering new continents, as

was the fashion at the time. But look closely at where his hands are going and why. Elsewhere he poetically takes the clothes off this woman:

> Your gown going off, such beauteous state reveals,
> As when from flowery meadows the hill's shadow steals.
> Off with that wiry Coronet and show
> The hairy diadem which on you doth grow:
> Now off with those shoes, and then softly tread
> In this, love's hallowed temple, this soft bed.

Examine the stunning opening of one of Emily Dickinson's tiny poems:

> I heard a Fly buzz—when I died—
> The Stillness in the Room
> Was like the Stillness in the Air—
> Between the Heaves of Storm

This poem is about timelessness—or time stopping. If we do feel anything at the moment of death, might it not be a deep-focus, almost microscopic view of the world around us? If you're not familiar or comfortable with poetry, don't be put off. For this exercise you're not looking for anything but your own pleasure. The capital letters Dickinson uses are a common feature of older poetry. The strange words *safeliest* and *empiree* that Donne uses are simply archaic. If you read these poems in a Norton anthology, you'll likely have notes to explain both historical phrases and obsolete words.

OLD AND NEW MEDIA

I like fiction that honestly takes account of the other media available to its readers. There is no need to be jealous of, or disoriented by, TV, film, the Internet, or newspapers. Read and comprehend all available information. Play with every piece of knowledge and detail of human interaction you come across. Take good notes of whatever you like—keep a notebook with you when you're watching TV or even in movie theaters. Observe the way these other media work—break the whole down into component parts and operating procedures.

--- **23** ---

MAPQUEST. Be a time traveler to 1985 or 1996. Notice how antiquated computers in 1997 movies look—even a few years after 1997. From your privileged view in the present moment, look back with fond disdain on the archaic and arcane technologies of another time. Write a short story about a person who is using a word processor (what we called desktop computers then) for the first time, or a cell phone, or a DVD player. 500 words.

YOU'RE LOST DRIVING AROUND in Boston, so you call your sister in San Francisco to look up directions on MapQuest.com. She happens to be sitting by her computer, as you know she will be. She tells you exactly where to turn, which streets are one-way, what the weather is like. Write about these novelties (the Internet, cell phones) if you have any memory of life before them, or even if you don't. Massive changes have taken place in our technologies in the last five years, ten years, one hundred years (you choose). I still remember the wonder caused by watching my first video-tape, *Christine*, the mediocre Stephen King novel turned into a mediocre film. It was not a mediocre experience to watch my friend Peter Behrens pause the movie so we could talk about something other than the ridiculous story in front of us. I'd never imagined being able to stop a movie midstream. Watching films suddenly seemed like reading a novel.

———————————————— **24**)————————————————

ODDVERTISING. Write a script for a TV commercial. Think up an interesting product to sell, and a set of unusual ways of promoting its value and viability. The script should be 400 words long or less. Now show us two friends who are watching this commercial on TV. Don't retell too much of the ad, just enough to show us that these people are indeed watching this ad. Listen to their conversation for a while, which may or may not have anything to do with the advertisement they've just witnessed (although I suspect the ad will have a subliminal effect on their conversation). All this should be about 750 words.

IN A RECENT TV COMMERCIAL, a psychiatric patient drones on and on in English about his problems to a shrink. Eventually, the doctor speaks, but in Croatian. The voice-over of the commercial says something like, "You don't need advice from a broker you can't understand, either." This sort of clever, quick, metonymic transition from one part of the story to the next is very common in TV advertising. A *metonym* is a term for one thing "applied to another with which it has become closely associated," according to M.H. Abrams, in *A Glossary of Literary Terms.* Examples he gives are Hollywood for the film industry or "the crown" for the queen. Advertising indulges in this process all the time, mostly for the sake of efficiency, but also because advertising is overwhelmingly a symbolic or sign-based system of informing us of the need to buy this or that thing.

In his book *The Conquest of Cool,* Thomas Frank describes the history of American advertising (from the 1950s and 1970s) and the way stodgy 1950s advertising transformed itself in the 1960s. Advertising was no less a great lie than it had ever been, but it was a much hipper lie. Frank points to one book as a benchmark. *The Gap* was co-written in 1967 by a middle-aged adman and his nephew who was attending Columbia University:

> Each makes an effort to enter the world of the other: the adman smokes dope, the college student attends a martini-soaked client lunch at the Four Seasons. What astounds a contemporary reader is the inversion of generational roles that takes place. Ernest Fladell, the adman, is strangely candid and seems genuinely interested in the life of the mysterious young. He compares marijuana, with unmodulated admiration, to the alcohol he usually consumes: "The kids are on an entirely different kick. Sex isn't the object, nor is the ability to let go. They have both in reasonably good supply. Their groove is to feel more, see, taste, hear, enjoy more." But Richard Lorber, the hip twenty-year-old, is scornful and condescending and impossibly pretentious, recommending "experiments in expanded consciousness" to strangers and declaring that his uncle can't really have enjoyed marijuana (which "Many of my friends consider ... to be an experience of sacred depth") properly after one try because "Pot is a learning experience and each time one turns on the effect is amazingly cumulative."

How does this excerpt relate to the exercise I'm suggesting you write? The background of something as simple as a throwaway ad on TV in a story you're working on can be much deeper than you think. The research you do to make this ad believable and an integral part of your fiction may take you off in useful and creative directions. Perhaps you'll find the heart of the story in this research and in this tiny story within a story.

—————————————————(**25**)—————————————————

PUBLIC ART. Think about the pleasures, problems, and procedures of getting a piece of public art accepted and installed (say in a town square or in any number of urban open spaces or even in the subway of the new airport). Do some research on the subject. The artist has to apply for the permit, perhaps enter in an open competition, which means writing up a ridiculous proposal for the art. Imagine how hard it would be to please a city council or a group of veterans or a mayor. Now imagine what it would be like to write a piece of public fiction. This can be any sort of story or fragment of fiction. Because it will be set in a public space, the piece will have to be very small. It will be something hundreds and thousands of strangers will visit and look at. It may be part of a piece of art or sculpture. How would this change your attitude toward writing the piece? If it were an Iraq War memorial, say, who is your audience and whom would you be writing about? Why would a story be useful under these circumstances? 250 words.

—————————————————(**26**)—————————————————

MY NEIGHBOR TOTORO. Watch *My Neighbor Totoro* twice (even if you've already seen it several times). *Totoro* is a lovely movie made by the great Japanese anime filmmaker Hayao Miyazaki. Take a small, un-important scene and dig deeply into it. See the next exercise, Reruns

(27), for my thoughts on the fact that so many of us have become used to watching films and TV shows again and again. *Totoro* is a perfect little movie, so I am not proposing that you wreck it in any way. Just slice the film or videotape and paste in another scene or set of scenes. This is a very humble exercise. Take the story of *Totoro* as seriously as you can. If you dislike the film, don't do this exercise. 500 words.

IN HIS REVIEW OF THE MOVIE for the *Onion*, Noel Murray says:

> The genteel, languid [film] *Totoro* seems at first slight and even soporific. The sliver of a story—about two girls who move to a small village with their father while their mother recovers from a life-threatening illness—never gets past first gear, and the hero-ines' few encounters with the mystical forest spirit Totoro hardly justify the movie's title. Yet *My Neighbor Totoro* may be the most enduring entry in Miyazaki's impressive filmography, because it's so particular about the nuances of human behavior and emotion. The movie stands up to rewatching, gaining in profundity.
>
> It's hard to pinpoint exactly what makes *Totoro* breathe. Maybe it's that the girls run, stumble, and daydream in ways that are familiar and notably unfussy. *My Neighbor Totoro* examines how a family crisis affects children, but Miyazaki keeps some dis-tance from the subject, standing back and watching the sisters be kids, preoccupied by schoolwork and chores. As for the rounded, furry, playful Totoro and his family of woodland sprites, Miyazaki treats them as benign but ultimately alien. Throughout the movie, Totoro adopts some human habits, like clutching an umbrella,

but the point is that while we respect and rely on nature, there's something uniquely touching about being human, with lives and habits so flawed and yet so beautiful.

An aside: The movie reviews in the *Onion* are a wonderful treasure.

27

RERUNS. Use a movie you know extremely well (and presumably love) and interlace it with your own life history. Retell the story of the movie, in fragments, and then tell some autobiographical (fictional or relatively accurate) story from your own life. You will probably find interesting connections between the film narrative and the story. 500 words.

WATCHING MOVIES OVER AND OVER AGAIN has become a common experience for people who grew up after the advent of VCRs. When I was a kid (born in 1956) the only movies shown often enough on TV to be able to quote from them were *The Wizard of Oz* and *It's a Wonderful Life*. Now local and cable broadcast stations repeat cult favorites three times a weekend and sometimes back-to-back; we have videos and DVDs; children grow up watching the same movies dozens, even hundreds, of times. What is the effect of this?

28

THE PINUP. Write an exercise about a couple of teenage girls who examine carefully, with some irritation but also with interest that surprises them, a couple of issues of *Playboy* magazine—their father's, their brother's, a boyfriend's. Use any other old-fashioned taboo magazine of that type, if you prefer. Decide when this happens. It will matter a great deal if the discovery is in 1965 or 2005.

When *Playboy* was relatively new, it might have been a shock for daughters to discover the magazine in their father's closet. By the late twentieth century, the shock effect would have worn off, but a teenage girl might be appalled that her boyfriend has a stash of the magazines—she might be insulted; she might be worried it would lead to harder stuff; or she might think it was a sign of how quaint his views of women were. Examine some old issues of the magazine. Write something of a female complaint (or appreciation) of this hardy journal. 750 words.

JOAN ACOCELLA, in the March 20, 2006, issue of the *New Yorker*, writes about the history of the images of the women in *Playboy* magazine:

> In the 1980s and thereafter, the artificiality only increased, as did that of all American mass media. The most obvious change is in the body, which has now been to the gym. Before, you could often see the Playmates sucking in their stomachs. Now they don't have to. The waist is nipped, the bottom tidy, and the breasts are a thing of wonder. The first mention of a "boob job" in *The Playmate Book* has to do with Miss April 1965, but, like hair coloring, breast enlargement underwent a change of meaning, and hence of design, in the 1970s and 1980s. At first, its purpose was to correct nature, and fool people into thinking that this was what nature made. But over time the augmented bosom became confessedly an artifice—a *Ding an sich* [thing in itself], and proud of it. By the 1980s, the Playmates' breasts are not just huge. Many are independent of the law of gravity; they point straight outward. One pair seems to point upward. Other features look equally

doctored. The pubic hair becomes elegantly barbered—the women favor a Vandyke—or, in a few cases, is removed altogether ... Miss March 1968 got into *Playboy* because her grandmother wrote to the magazine, "My granddaughter is much better looking and much bustier than any of the girls you've been shooting."

I like Acocella's unprissy and relaxed reading of these images over the years (which is not to say she doesn't express horror at the wholesale reconstruction of these female bodies).

29

THE SHOUTING PHASE OF SITCOMS. Write a new script for part of an old favorite sitcom episode. I mean that the script should lay new dialogue over the old episode. Watch the show without sound several times. Calibrate your character's speeches to the show. Use the names of the characters in the show in your first draft of this experiment. In the second draft, change the names to names of your own fictional characters—from another story, a novel you're working on, or newly minted characters. 750 words.

WE ARE STILL A SITCOMMUNIST COUNTRY, though situation comedies are most definitely on the wane. The shouting phase of sitcoms is the third or fourth year of the run, when all the characters tend to yell at each other. Only *Seinfeld* managed to rescue itself from this phase, in the last few years, when the characters began to speak in indoor voices to each other again. *Sex and the City* had no laugh track (one of its more revolutionary features), and it did not go through a shouting phase. The laugh track was invented to stand in for the studio audience. *M*A*S*H* experimented with dropping it, but few other sitcoms dared go that way until studio audiences were rein-troduced (and occasionally amplified by surreptitious laugh tracks).

— 30)——————

BLOGS. Read a blog, preferably not a well-known blog. It could be someone's personal, interesting, bracingly honest, silly, or completely self-involved blog. Read the blog for a few days. Get used to the personal tics and characteris-tics of this voice. You might want to look at several blogs in order to collect a larger folder of vocal mannerisms. When you feel you know this material well, write in this person's voice (or in an amalgamation of different voices). What you will write for this exercise is not another blog, but a comment to an online version of a newspaper or magazine article (something in *Salon*, *Newsweek*, or the *Washington Post*, for example). Thousands of people do this. The com-ment should be fairly short. What you're looking to discover in this exercise is another voice, a unique way of apprehending the world. 250 words.

NOAM COHEN, IN THE *NEW YORK TIMES*, wrote about one of the great politi-cal blogs, *Talking Points Memo*, which won a prize for journalism in 2008 (but not the Pulitzer). He and others in the mainstream media have often expressed alarm at the world of blogs and online reporting. Cohen talks to another authority to give his own piece extra authority:

> Dan Kennedy, a media critic who teaches at Northeastern University, has followed *Talking Points Memo* from its inception. What *Talking Points Memo* does, he said, "is a different kind of journalism, based on the idea that my readers know more than I do." Markos Moulitsas (founder of the Web site *Daily Kos*) predicted, "It may take a decade,

but Josh Marshall will win a Pulitzer some day." It won't be this year. Sig Gissler, the administrator of the Pulitzer Prizes, said in an e-mail message that online articles are eligible for the awards, but they must have been published on a weekly or daily newspaper's Web site. "A freestanding Web site does not qualify," he said.

31

OLD NEWS. Write about someone who has been the subject of an erroneous description in a newspaper. This person is not an important figure—not a politician or athlete or movie star. She was simply incorrectly quoted, in a way that embarrasses the person (and reveals this character to be something other than the character thinks herself to be). Your exercise should be a study of what happens to a person wronged this way, not about the mechanics of getting a newspaper or reporter to admit error. Imagine what it's like to feel publicly wronged by an entity that cares about the truth but cares more about tomorrow's truths. 500 words.

IN *SLATE*, DAHLIA LITHWICK EXCORIATED Nancy Grace, a CNN talking head, who interviewed the mother of a boy who'd gone missing. Grace hectored the mother in a phone interview (for not taking a lie detector test, which her lawyer told her not to do), and shortly afterwards the mother killed herself. Lithwick notes:

> [Among Nancy] Grace's most revealing statements, as she struggled to disavow any responsibility for Duckett's death this week, was this one: "I do not feel our show is to blame for what happened to Melinda Duckett," Grace said Monday. "Melinda committed suicide

before that interview ever aired." It speaks volumes about Grace's worldview that in her mind, reality doesn't happen until and unless it's witnessed by her viewers. By the same token, she seems to believe there is no real justice until it happens on her show.

I once heard the story of a newspaper reporter who had maligned someone in his paper. The next day he dismissed the charge of libel by saying that this was old news, and old news, by definition, is not news at all.

─────────────── **32** ───────────────

LIES OF THE PRESS. Henry Adams, in a letter in 1862, said, "The press is the hired agent of a monied system and set up for no other purpose than to tell lies where the interests [of the wealthy] are involved." Whether or not you believe this, write a very short story in the form of a part of an article in a newspaper that includes a large lie meant to cover up for big business or governmental malfeasance. Use the newspaper method of two columns of print per page. 500 words.

WALTER BENJAMIN, IN HIS ESSAY on Karl Kraus, an early twentieth-century antijournalism journalist, an aphorist, and generally a rabble-rouser, shows us how Kraus portrays the typical journalist:

> [He is] "a person who has little interest either in himself and his own existence, or in the mere existence of things, but who feels things only in their relationships, above all where these meet in events—and only in this moment become united, substantial, and alive" ... In the end [Kraus] brought together all his energies in the struggle against the empty phrase, which is the linguistic expres-

sion of the despotism with which, in journalism, topicality sets up its dominion over things.

What Benjamin means is that newspapers (and now TV news) measure their interest in what is happening only by what is of "interest" at the current moment. The news industry has always had a distrust of history. Kraus and Benjamin both see the great drawback of a newspaper that has to produce one (or more) editions a day (or a magazine that produces one a week or one a month) as inimical to real understanding of the world around us. In contemporary terms, this translates to the horse-race mentality of reporters about presidential campaigns. Who is ahead now? Okay, a month later, who is pulling up neck and neck with the front-runner? The narrative of politics—or of any news "story"—becomes more important than explaining it. Fox News (which is only the latest example of partisan news sources) has influenced all news reporters to think in terms of presenting several sides to each political story (and political stories have come to include reporting on hard science, amazingly). If every story has two sides, there can be no right or wrong. The right wing in the United States has complained long and hard about what they call relativism, the very idea that there is no one single truth, but they take advantage of relativism in their own cynical ways.

33

THE HAPPY BOY AND HIS FAMILY. In Japan, *Leave It to Beaver* is called *The Happy Boy and His Family*. Imagine someone in another country watching an American sitcom—a Japanese boy watching *The Andy Griffith Show*, a trio of Swedish teenage girls watching *Seinfeld*. The activity of this exercise will have little to do with the story on the TV screen, but you may have to do more work to describe and imagine yourself into this alternate world (unless you're Japanese or Swedish). But try to convey some of the interesting mistranslations. Make them up. 500 words.

IN 1969, MY FAMILY OF FIVE had flown to Stockholm. I'd never been out of the country, except to Canada, which was another kind of home because my grandparents lived there. I was a young teen, a big boy, tough and surly. We all slept for eleven hours that first night. I woke up first and went downstairs to the living room of the apartment we were borrowing from friends of friends. I turned on the TV. The show, at the moment, was very familiar, *I Love Lucy*, but it was immediately clear it was wrong—it was dubbed into Swedish, this barbaric, knotted language. I started to cry quietly. After a moment I began to sob until my mother came into the room and asked what was wrong. I could not tell her.

34

HEADLESS BODY IN TOPLESS BAR. Go through your local newspaper—maybe a half dozen papers over a few weeks. Look for interesting, funny headlines. Write them down. Build up a file of these odd lines that aren't sentences (usually). When you've collected fifteen of them, try to arrange them in some kind of logical order. You may have to cut out some of the fifteen. Fill in your own sentences (one or two or three) between these headlines. These sentences should not be headline-type writing, but be faithful to whatever weird story is being built by this arrangement of thought. 500 words.

THE *NEW YORK POST* RAN THIS HEADLINE in 1982: "Headless Body in Topless Bar." It is perhaps the most famous tabloid headline of all time. Stephen Metcalf, in *Slate*, analyzed the way this species of newspaper works:

> The *New York Post* is designed to tingle the lizard brain of its read-
> ers, via one button labeled "Prurience," a second labeled "Outrage,"
> all to no greater purpose than to further the ambitions of its owner,
> Rupert Murdoch, and to fill my infrequent subway rides from
> Brooklyn into Manhattan with some kitschy distraction. Unlike the
> *Times*, the *Post* has no reputation to guard, save one: Its sports
> page is hands-down the best in the city. It delivers exactly what the
> sports consumer most craves—i.e., rumor, innuendo, supposition,
> and scurrilous gossip. Above all, it delivers opinion, not with the
> white-glove judiciousness of the Gray Lady but with the barstool
> surety of a delightful, irresponsible, and thoroughly knowledgeable
> drunk. Among the New York sports opinionati, the back page of the
> *Post* operates as a kind of final verdict. Is your favorite slugger a Boy
> Scout or a philanderer? A stalwart or a crybaby? A hero or a bum?
> We report; we decide.

35

THE DEVIOUS LIE OF A SNAPSHOT. Take old snapshots of yours—or digital photos on your computer. Or go to flickr.com and look at other people's personal photographs. Try to read the image as clearly and logi-cally as you can—but not honestly. There is no way to decipher the mean-ing of a photo, just as the 9/11 image referenced below cannot be parsed for moral or ethical meaning. Write a small amount of prose about six different photographs—no more than 200 words for each photograph. Put the writing away for a few days. When you return to this collection of prose, choose four or five of the best paragraphs. Put them together in useful and interesting order. Work on them, reduce, expand, go off on tangents. Your final product should be less than 750 words.

THOMAS HOEPKER TOOK a famous and controversial photograph on September 11, 2001, which shows five young people sitting near New York Harbor in Brooklyn Heights, talking casually, with the smoke rising from the devastation of the destruction of the World Trade Center. Here is a link to a *Slate* magazine article about this photo and its controversy (with the image part way down the page): www.slate.com/id/2149675. Here are Louis P. Masur's comments on the photograph in the *Chronicle of Higher Education*, November 23, 2007:

> Hoepker [said] "the image has touched many people exactly because it remains fuzzy and ambiguous in all its sun-drenched sharpness," especially five years after the event. He wondered, was the picture "just the devious lie of a snapshot, which ignored the seconds before and after I had clicked the shutter?"

"The devious lie of a snapshot" is a marvelous phrase. It is not the photographer who is devious, but the nature of the snapshot itself, which isolates and freezes action, disconnecting it from context and sequence. Photographs seduce us into believing that they are objective records, but, in fact, all images are interpretations, texts that must be read.

What every photographer captures is of the moment and beyond it, random and in odd ways determined, fixed yet always changing. Amateurs and professionals alike bring to the camera a life immersed in images. When one of their pictures becomes a cultural icon, it is because it is original but also commonplace, unique yet somehow familiar. The best photographs inform and move us. They allow us to enter a frozen instant of time and somehow make it our own.

— 36)——————

THE PARTY. Write a short short story about the photograph below, "Party in the Tot Yard," which was taken by Dan Weiner in 1953 in Park Forest, Illinois. 500 words.

— 37)——————

SON OF A PREACHER MAN. Write a fragment of a story that largely or slightly concerns a popular song that tells a good story. This is a rare phenomenon—songs with good stories—so look hard. First of all, write a prose summary of the story of your song, in your own words as much as possible. You can integrate this summary into the story fragment, or just use parts of it. Quote from the song, from time to time. Also, misquote, if you're feeling frisky (like the lyrics from a Bruce Springsteen song I misheard years ago, "Ripped off like a douche in the middle of the night"). 500 words.

THE SONG "SON OF A PREACHER MAN" was written by John Hurley and Ronnie Wilkins and first sung by Dusty Springfield. The way Dusty Springfield sings about Billy-Ray, who was "a preacher's son," is unusual, sensual, and excited. The "story" of the song is simple. Billy-Ray's father would visit her house and the menfolk would begin to talk, which was a signal for the son to take the singer of the song out for a walk. She says Billy-Ray was "the only one who could ever reach me," as if this surprised her. The climax of the song goes like this:

> Being good isn't always easy,
> No matter how hard I tried,
> When he started sweet talking to me,
> he'd come tell me everything is alright,
> he'd kiss and tell me everything is alright,
> Can I get away again tonight?

Note the way story works in this song. The line that opens the third stanza, "Being good isn't always easy," telegraphs the moral tension of the song. The last line of the song, "Can I get away again tonight?" indicates there has been a good deal more sexual play going on than the surface of the lyrics in the story would have us believe. This was written in the late

1960s, a somewhat more innocent time in American culture. The song was given to Aretha Franklin and she turned it down. She did record the song later, after Dusty Springfield's hit, but it was never included on an Aretha Franklin album, perhaps because it was too direct, despite these lacunae I mentioned. A *lacuna* is a blank space or a missing part (originally from the same word as *lagoon*). The story in "Son of a Preacher Man" is apparently casual, without incident—no murder, rape, sexual activity. It is full of yearning. The fact that this was the son of a minister would seem to indicate chastity and earnestness. But the line "Yes he was, he was, oh yes he was," shows something else. Children of psychiatrists have a reputation for being a bit loony. Children of preachers have a reputation, whether deserved or not, for being wild.

---- 38)----

BEVERLY SILLS. Read the two paragraphs below from Beverly Sills's obituary in *Newsweek*. What interests me in these two paragraphs is the description of Sills's change as a singer and artist when she returned to the stage after the birth of her children. Imagine a character who is an artist—opera singer, sculptor, stand-up comic. Visit this character that has experienced a tragedy or set of tragedies and had to give up his art for a time. Visit this character after the return to the artistic activity. Show us the process of preparing for the art (rehearsal or preparing a canvas) rather than the actual performance of the art itself. 500 words.

HERE IS SOME OF KATRINE AMES'S OBITUARY of Beverly Sills (born Belle Silverman of Brooklyn, New York, in 1929, the same year as my mother, who was also an opera singer) from *Newsweek*:

At her peak in the 1960s and 1970s, she could float passages over a full orchestra; she could sing long runs in which each individual note was clear but which ran down a listener's back like melted chocolate. She had a trill that could wind a clock, and could color her voice from shimmering silver or almost transparent blue to dark red.

Her professional life was often triumphant; her personal life, far less so. She was happily married to Peter Greenough, a former newspaper columnist who died last year, for almost fifty years, but their daughter, Meredith, is profoundly deaf and their son, Peter Jr., is severely retarded and autistic. Before the births of her children, Sills had always been a good, dependable singer. But after taking a leave of absence to be with them, she came back a different artist. Her only worry-free moments, she said, were when she was onstage, and the stage was her liberator. She became artistically fearless, and she tore through the musical world.

39

THE CONCEPT ALBUM. Write an essay about several different drafts of a story you've been working on for a long time. As you write this essay, you may drift into storytelling mode, but don't worry. Maintain the stance of an essayist as long as possible. Cut and paste parts of the story into this essay, but always present them as quotations, isolated examples of a point you're trying to make. Summarize and paraphrase from the previous drafts as well. Be critical. Even if you can't think of tough, damning things to say about your own story, make them up, pretend to be someone else writing about your fiction. Slowly, I think you'll begin to find you've written another draft of this story. 1,000 words.

In "Why Listening Will Never Be the Same," Terry Teachout talks about this revolution in making music, the concept album:

> Such famous albums as Glenn Gould's 1955 recording of the Bach Goldberg Variations, Frank Sinatra's *Only the Lonely*, Miles Davis's *Kind of Blue*, or the Beatles' *Sgt. Pepper's Lonely Hearts Club Band* are not attempts to simulate live performances. They are, rather, unique experiences existing only on record, and the record itself, not the music or the performance, is the art object.

The concept album was not built out of one continuous live performance. I'm not suggesting that *Sgt. Pepper* or *Kind of Blue* are trying to act as if they weren't albums of musical expression, but they did not care to sound like one continuous session—a set of music played in the smoky basement of some Hamburg bar. The fact that musicians began to build sounds, put together parts and pieces of music with other parts and pieces of music to create a continuous whole, is something like what the postmodern fiction writers did in the 1960s, but also many writers long before that period. Fiction for a long time was supposed to feel natural, unconstructed, "realistic," as if it weren't fiction. Glenn Gould is perhaps the most unlikely of these musicians to have wanted to make music out of fragments (though it is also surprising to see jazz musician Miles Davis among this group—jazz by its very nature is supposed to be impressionistic, full of feeling, personal, not artificial and built).

LANGUAGE GAMES

What I mean for you to do in these exercises is to take apart words and sentences and rebuild them with simple and arbitrary rules for their reconstruction. This is something like the concept the philosopher Ludwig Wittgenstein spoke of in *The Blue and Brown Books*. Wittgenstein's language-games, according to *The Penguin Dictionary of Critical Theory*, were:

> [A] way of using signs that is simpler than that in which the signs of everyday language are used, and [he] contends both that language-games are the forms of language with which children first make use of words and that they are primitive forms of language.

Nick Hornby, in the *Believer*, quotes Francis Spufford in his memoir *The Child That Books Built* (which gives us a rare lyrical glimpse at the process of learning how to read):

> When I caught the mumps, I couldn't read; when I went back to school again, I could. The first page of *The Hobbit* was a thicket of symbols, to be decoded one at a time and joined hesitantly together ... By the time I reached *The Hobbit*'s last page, though, writing had softened, and lost the outlines of the printed alphabet, and become a transparent liquid, first viscous and sluggish, like a jelly of meaning, then ever thinner and more mobile, flowing faster and faster, until it reached me at the speed of thinking and I could not entirely distinguish the suggestions it was making from my own thoughts. I had undergone the acceleration into the written word that you also experience as a change in the medium. In fact, writing had ceased to be a thing—an

object in the world—and *become* a medium, a substance you look through.

In these exercises, try to approximate the wonder you first felt when you conquered reading.

———————————— **40**)————————————

ANAGRAMS. An anagram is a word or phrase that contains *all* the letters of another word or phrase in a different order. The phrase *no more stars* is an anagram of *astronomers*. Pick an important word and use it for the title of a small fragment of fiction. For example, you might play with the word *surrealism*. If you're stuck or just not good at this game, go to this site (http://wordsmith.org/anagram/), which spits out anagrams of words or phrases with lightning speed (and it gives you way too many choices, so you still have some work to do to pick and choose among the choices). *Surrealism* has the following anagrams: *serial rums, liar's serum, rural semis, Sir A.M. rules,* and *Sierra slum*.

Think about the word itself as a dominating presence in the story. It might be better to use a phrase like *surrealism is dreamy* or *surrealism is contradictory*. In any case, choose a long word with a variety of letters for this exercise. When you've collected a few of these anagrams, work them into their own set of sentences and phrases, without trying to write a story or make larger sense. Once you've got a dozen or more sentences put together, examine what you have and what it may mean. Meaning, in this case, is a relative thing. You can find meaning in any set of random objects or words. The meaning you find will probably come from your own unconscious mind (from buried memories or events you think were completely unconnected to each other), so relax and be playful or ridiculous. Let yourself wander aimlessly into a story. 500 words.

THE WORD YOU CHOOSE not only should be capable of making interesting anagrams, but it should mean something to you. I chose *surrealism* because I am slyly connecting this exercise to that early twentieth-century movement, which tried to reach the subconscious mind by juxtaposing ideas that seem to contradict each other. The word or phrase you choose should already have a connection to your own history or intellectual development. My father is Canadian and I grew up in one stable small town in western Massachusetts, but travel and restlessness have marked my life. I could see myself exploring the phrase *displaced person* in this exercise. My phrase is *prances lopsided*, and contains *a splendid corpse* (the italicized words are the anagrams). What you're looking for in this writing is a beautiful piece of poem-shaped prose.

41

CONCORDANCE. Pick two books you like and know well that have concordances on Amazon.com (see below). Write an exercise using only these words as your vocabulary. Let the words guide you toward the subject of this fragment of fiction—see if you can find, independent of the novels, the sort of content and mood this piece of narrative should have. 500 words.

I'M NOT SURE WHY, but Amazon has a feature called a Concordance in books marked with the Search Inside tool (just navigate to a book's main page, hover over the cover image with the Search Inside tag, and you'll see a pop-up box called Inside This Book). A *concordance* is the alphabetical index of the 100 principal words in a book (or the works of an author). Here is the concordance of my own novel, *I Know Many Songs, But I Cannot Sing*:

> across again against American another Arabic arm asks away balcony building Cairo call chair Charles city come daughter day does door down Egypt Egyptian English European even eyes face feels few first friend Gamal girl go going good hand head himself home hour ib ih know language last laughs Ib Lena lights long look man men moment name next night now old own people prisoner read right room Ruqayyah Safeyya say saying see sits small something speak stands still story street table take talk tell thing think three time told turns two walks want wife without woman word years Yehya

and here's the concordance of James Joyce's *Ulysses*:

> again always arms asked away behind bit black Bloom call came come course day Dedalus door down ever eyes face father fellow first get girl give go god going good got hand hat head heart high himself house Joe John know last left let life little long look lord love man men might mother Mr Mulligan must name new night now old own place poor put right round saw say see sir something Stephen still street take tell thing think though thought three time told took two voice want water went white wife without woman words world years yes young

---------------------------------(42)----------------------------------

ENCYCLOPEDIAS. Write a fake encyclopedia entry for several pre-existing characters of yours, as if they were well known and well liked. You could also write an encyclopedia entry for one of your character's inventions or famous battles or sensational murders. What makes an encyclopedia's voice so oracular? Study examples, particularly less impressive ones than *Encyclopedia Britannica* (but look at that old standard, too). 750 words.

HUGH KENNER, in *Flaubert, Joyce and Beckett: The Stoic Comedians*, says, "The novel has an encyclopedic capacity for fact." Kenner also points out that the novel, with Flaubert, began to parody itself. Emma Bovary reads and tries to *live* bad fiction of the recent age with tragic and pathetic consequences. By the late nineteenth century, the novel became deeply aware of itself, showing its edges, bindings, and boundaries as art. In *The Stoic Comedians*, Kenner notices that the novel and the encyclopedia travel alongside each other in Flaubert and Joyce. The encyclopedia, unlike the novel, makes no pretense of overarching, organic sense, and it has no literary precursors. Dictionaries and encyclopedias arrived with the invention of print and the idea of the book. The first encyclopedia made cross-references to entries that did not yet exist, an indication of the open-endedness of the form.

Kenner also observes that the branch of the novel that flows from Flaubert is very concerned with the page, with echoing itself, and with language that can only be read, not recited. The novel, by the late nineteenth century, was completely a book. Before this development, it pretended to be something else—a message in a bottle, a set of letters, a dream of life something like the later technology of film. For Flaubert, the novel was only and exquisitely something read, written, and referring back on and to itself.

_____ 43)_____

250 DIFFERENT WORDS. Write a 250-word story in which you never use the same word twice—each of the 250 words is *different*. You may not use a variation of a word, like *you'll* after you've already used *you*. In this instruction I've already used *in*, *you*, *use*, *word*, *the*, and *250* more than once.

For this exercise, you should also come up with a hidden title, something that also follows the rules of the story (meaning these extra words cannot be repeated in the body of the story and cannot have repetitions within them). You may want to make the hidden title first, or do it after you've done a draft of the story. Why employ a hidden title? Many stories and novels, for all we know, have this sort of underground foundation. The effect of the hidden title will be to guide you toward or away from it (or parallel to it). The central instruction for this piece, though, will be incredibly difficult all by itself, so I wouldn't worry too much about the title, hidden or otherwise. By the way, just because you have a hidden title doesn't mean you cannot also have an unhidden title.

The difficulty of these instructions is the defining characteristic of this task. It will be nearly impossible to make a coherent story with this set of restrictions, but it will also challenge you to invent a method entirely different than anything you've used before. Don't expect fluency. Assume words will come out two or three at a time. Try not to search for synonyms. Rearrange a whole sentence if necessary. When you make expression symbolically difficult this way, you are in effect teaching yourself your own language again.

44

RECUPERATION. Take an old story of yours—a successful story or a failure, it doesn't matter. Erase 95 percent of the story. In a 1,500-word story, that would leave you with 75 words. Choose which 75 words you'll keep very carefully. Maintain the order of the words from the original piece of fiction, then fill in about half as many words between these 75 words (for example). Once you've begun to find a new story, you need no longer worry about the order of the original 75 words. Your final draft should be no more than 500 words.

I CALLED AN EARLY TITLE of this exercise Erasure, but this is more like performing CPR on a piece of fiction. In your old fiction, you are looking for essential problems and themes you may not have known obsessed you. All fiction writing should be a process somewhat like this recuperation. You explore your own inner demons and desires, setting up alternate situations and scenarios—alternatives to your own lived life.

Karla Kelsey, the author of *Knowledge, Forms, the Aviary*, has done something like this exercise in her poetry.

45

TRANSLATION FROM THE SAME LANGUAGE. Take someone else's very short story (three pages or less)—Isaac Babel, Grace Paley, Diane

Williams, Ernest Hemingway, Lydia Davis, Edgar Allan Poe. Behave as if this story were written in a foreign tongue. Change every word from the original. You need not keep the same number of sentences or words per sentence. Also change the proper names of characters and places. This may sound like a complete transformation of the target story, but keep in mind the notion that you are indeed translating from one language to another, attempting to keep something of the spirit of the original. The length will depend on the story you choose to translate.

THIS EXERCISE IS like the exercise Logical Structure from *The 3 A.M. Epiphany*, but it differs in one crucial aspect: You will be redoing an entire short short story. You will take someone else's whole construction and try to understand it (but you may not completely understand it—that's okay). And you will make it into your own fiction.

46

SUBSTITUTION. Take the name of an old friend—someone living or dead. Put this name into a brief story set in a time well before this friend was born. You may want to give this fictional character some traits of your friend, but all you should worry about in this exercise is the simple substitution of your friend's name. The effect is to make history intimate and give life to this friend's name in another moment in time. 500 words.

I WROTE TWO STORIES ABOUT WORLD WAR II for my novel *The River Gods*. In one, a Japanese soldier and an American GI have mortally wounded each other, and they are lying on the ground very near one another. I used the name of a friend of mine in place of this soldier. My friend Tom Andrews died in 2001 in his late thirties. He was a poet and colleague of mine at Ohio University. I used a small piece of an essay Tom wrote on poetry to describe the process of dying. This was both chilling and invigorating— so simply fictionalizing a factual story. In the other story, set in Egypt at the beginning of the war and before the Americans really joined in the battles in North Africa, I used the name of my old high school friend Gary O'Dea, who died a year after we all graduated from college. He was the first person my own age I knew well who died.

— 47)

INDEX. Take a nonfiction book you love that has a good, long index. It should be history or sociology or philosophy. Browse the index. Type up large chunks of the index that grab your interest. When you've got a good list of phrases from this book, go through and prune, selecting only the phrases you are most drawn to. When you've got a list of about twenty entries, go to the pages in the book where these phrases appear. Read around the phrases, and find a few other phrases, as well as the one put in the index, which are pleasurable. Type up these phrases into one continuous paragraph. Let this amalgamation of thoughts, radically wrested from this book, sit for a long while on your computer. After a few weeks or even months, go back to this wad of prose and rewrite it dramatically, energetically, with the spirit of a fiction writer, not a philosopher or scientist or social scientist. 750 words.

— 48)

AUTOMATIC WRITING. Employ the practice of automatic writing to create a small fragment of writing on any topic your unconscious mind wishes or wills. Despite the efforts you should make to free your mind completely of any preordained thoughts or notions about what you'll write, give your unconscious thoughts a little shove. If you're writing a novel or a story, read some part of it very carefully before you embark on the process of automatic writing (but provide a break of mind between the reading and the writing—do some meditation, go for a walk, take a shower).

Here is my notion of how to do automatic writing: Clear your desk. Use a pen or pencil you're comfortable with, which is your normal writing instrument. Place a blank sheet of paper in front of you. Turn off the lights and close the blinds (it's better to do this at night—the spirits are more apt to be at home in the dark). Feel the paper with both hands. Write with both hands, but you should not be able to see what you're writing. Write, and keep writing without any thoughts, until you feel you've filled the page. Try not to think about what you're writing while you write. Don't look at what you've written when you turn the lights on again, and put the paper in a drawer for a few days. Go back to this sheet of paper and use it however you wish. There is no word limit for the automatic writing itself, but when you go back to it for revision, your finished product should be no more than 500 words.

IN THE EARLY PART OF THE TWENTIETH CENTURY, the Surrealists pioneered the use of automatic writing for poetry. Charles Simic describes an encounter between the Mexican poet Octavio Paz and one of the founders of the Surrealist movement, André Breton, in Simic's book of essays and memoirs, *The Unemployed Fortune-Teller*:

> Octavio Paz ... told me [a] story about going to visit André Breton
> in Paris after the War. He was admitted and told to wait because

the poet was engaged. Indeed, from the living room where he was seated, he could see Breton writing furiously in his study. After a while he came out, and they greeted each other and set out to have lunch in a nearby restaurant.

"What were you working on, *maître?*" Paz inquired as they were strolling to their destination.

"I was doing some automatic writing," Breton replied.

"But," Paz exclaimed in astonishment, "I saw you erase repeatedly!"

"It was not automatic enough," Breton assured the young poet.

49

WEEKLY EXERCISE. Write a piece of fiction over a year. Make it fifty-two sentences long. Write one sentence a week. Work on this sentence very carefully. Don't plan the next sentence when you're working on this one sentence. You can and should certainly look back at your previous sentences. The subject of the story should be in part the passage of one year and whatever changes this year has wrought on a handful of fictional characters. There is no word limit for this exercise, but stick to fifty-two sentences.

ALGORITHMS

I have sometimes called the exercises in this book and in *The 3 A.M. Epiphany* creative algorithms. The phrase *probabilistic algorithms*, which are procedures that incorporate randomness, best describes what writers try to do before they've started writing fiction. Most writers work without an outline, but you can enhance your own ability to design the shape and organization of your fiction without constructing overly deterministic and perhaps creativity-killing outlines or plans.

On a very large scale—a lifetime—one can also discern simple algorithms layered over a writer's or artist's body of work. The artist Robert Rauschenberg grew up very poor in Port Arthur, Texas. His mother made most of her children's clothes. She even remade the suit her younger brother would have been buried in (had she not liberated it) into a skirt for herself. Rauschenberg probably did not connect this, at first, to his own use of ordinary material at hand to make his art, but it is one of the characteristic practices of his own artistic career—the readymade. Even more simply, the sculptor Henry Moore's mother had a bad back, and all through his childhood he massaged her torso from the hips to the shoulders. This view of his mother became his view of all human beings. His sculptures often look as if they were seen by a small child looking up at a giant adult.

_____(**50**)_____

FACT AND FANCY REVERSED. In *The 3 A.M. Epiphany* I wrote an exercise called Fact and Fancy. Here are the instructions for that exercise:

> Write a brief autobiographical story or fragment in which you use alternating objective and personal sentences. One sentence should set down relatively objective, factual details, focused and clear-headed, without bias or interpretation. The next sentence should be personal opinion; it should reveal feeling—deep or shallow; it

should respond to the factual sentence but need not respond directly. Alternate like this. Write a total of thirty sentences—fifteen objective, fifteen personal.

In this exercise, reverse the qualities of each sentence type. Tell the factual sentences emotionally and the emotional stuff in cool, objective language.

IF YOU GIVE YOURSELF NARRATIVE LICENSE to indulge in hidden exclamation points at the ends of these sentences, you'll find an unusual way of maneuvering through these minefields. And the emotion-filled sentences told in an even tone, without excess or adjectival madness, might have the effect of heightening the intensity of these thoughts or narrative descriptions. How do you do this?

My mother died in my arms after the ricochet gunshot wound to her thigh, which should not have killed her, but the bullet from my gun hit an artery and the blood blew out of the hole like a garden hose.

Or

The integrity of sauce was compromised when the sous-chef let it boil too long and too hard, forming suppurating clots and out-gassing a greasy musky odor you don't ever want emanating from this light smooth roux.

51

NO MIDDLE, TWO ENDINGS. Write a short story with no beginning, two middles, and three endings. Or write a narrative with two beginnings, no middle, and two endings. How will this work? Two endings may mean two alternate endings, or it may mean you present one false ending and another definitive ending. In the movie *Alien,* Sigourney Weaver's Ripley seems safely aboard her escape ship, the last survivor of the *Nostromo.* But it turns out the alien has stowed away with Ripley and the cat Jones— another ending, and a common tactic in horror movies (or think of Carrie's hand rising up through the gravel, which is all that's left of her house, at the end of Brian De Palma's movie *Carrie*). 750 words.

—————————————(52)—————————————

APHORISMS. Collect a dozen aphorisms. Make up your own. Scour encyclopedias of aphorisms or epigrams (*The Penguin Dictionary of Epigrams,* for example). It is important that half of the aphorisms you use in this exercise are those you made up yourself. Once you've got a good collection, populate a scene with a handful of friends talking over an unimportant subject. Let your characters speak these epigrams intermittently. Perhaps two of the characters speak all of the aphorisms, and the other characters speak only their original thoughts. When your people speak these pithy remarks they should not note the source. See what happens to your conversation when you deliberately spice it up with dense thought like this. Let the quality of the aphorisms leak into the other speeches. 500 words.

KARL KRAUS SAID, "It is often difficult to write an aphorism if you know how to do it. It is much easier if you don't." Kraus was a master of this kind of aphorism, but there is a telling simplicity to his description of the process. According to the *Online Etymology Dictionary* (www.etymonline.com), the word comes from "to mark off or divide," and an "*aphorism* is a short, pithy statement containing a truth of general import." Here are some definitions of its near-synonyms, also from the *Etymology Dictionary*: "an *axiom* is a statement of self-evident truth; a *theorem* is a demonstrable proposition in science or mathematics; an *epigram* is like an aphorism, but lacking in general import. *Maxim* and *saying* can be used as synonyms for *aphorism*." So the effective definition of an aphorism is that it is more art than truth. Keep in mind the art and the common mirror-like structure of aphorisms (see Benjamin Franklin's saying below).

Here are a few examples of aphorisms:

Digressions, objections, delight in mockery, carefree mistrust are signs of health; everything unconditional belongs in pathology. (Nietzsche)

When choosing between evils, I always like to take the one I've never tried before. (Mae West)

When I'm good, I'm very good. But when I'm bad, I'm better. (Mae West)

By failing to prepare, you are preparing to fail. (Benjamin Franklin)

By means of shrewd lies, unremittingly repeated, it is possible to make people believe that heaven is hell—and hell heaven. The greater the lie, the more readily it will be believed. (Adolf Hitler)

53

COUNTRY NOISES. Write a short scene in which a visual explanation of a sound is crucial to the moment. This means you will have to listen to some particular sound for a while and then do a simple drawing of the sound. Do this many times with different sounds. Then try to approximate what these visual images look like in words. Your characters could be whispering to each other. They might be in danger. They need desperately to impart to each other the details of these sounds. 500 words.

SAUL STEINBERG ONCE DID A LOVELY DRAWING, "Country Noises," for the *New Yorker*. Here are some of my own versions of these visual cues to what sounds look like:

Leaf blower six blocks away

〜〜〜〜〜〜〜〜〜〜 Jet from Denver to Pittsburgh in WaKeeney, Kansas

••• ⬜⬜ •• ⬜⬜⬜ •• •• ⬜⬜⬜⬜ •• ⬜⬜ •• ⬜ •••• ⬜⬜ • • Corn snow

Corn snow is large-grained, rounded crystals formed by the repeated melting and freezing of snow. Other country noises Saul Steinberg did graphic representations of are a chest of drawers creaking; a phone ringing; a furnace; a refrigerator; rain on a roof; rain on a deck; a willow branch lightly scratching against a window at three in the morning. From just these simple phrases I hope you can imagine lovely sonic images.

―――――――――― **54**)―――――――――――

COINCIDENCE. Write a narrative with a big coincidence in it. The coincidence should be fairly obvious and the center of your fragment of a story. Explore as many of its ramifications as you can (don't be shy to explain why it is a surprising thing). Coincidences seem to indicate an order beyond our rational understanding of how the world works, which is perhaps why they fell out of favor with the Modernists. 750 words.

AN AMERICAN TEENAGER IS WALKING across a square in Lyon, France, and she sees her best friend from fourth grade, whom she hasn't seen in five years, fifty yards away. An eleven-year-old boy is hit in the chest by a line drive at a baseball game. His heart stops. A nurse in the stands a few seats away administers CPR and saves his life. Seven years later, the boy is a dishwasher in a restaurant, but he is also a volunteer fireman, and a woman in the restaurant begins to choke on a hot dog. The boy administers CPR and saves her life. She is the nurse who saved his life seven years before. These are coincidences. They happen all the time. Another reason fiction has shied away from them for the last century is because coincidences seemed to be authorial meddling. But if the coincidence is at the heart of a story, not a means of wrapping up the plot, it might be more viable and effective.

55

RECYCLING. Take ten pieces of prose from at least five different sources—cereal boxes, newspapers, instructions for use in a medicine package, billboards, car manual information. Each piece of prose should be at least 20 words long and no more than 40 words long. Use this language as raw material for a fragment of fiction about a person who hoards things, who cannot throw anything out. This character is insane. In many other ways, he functions well. He just can't let go of possessions, but these pieces of writing you have collected are not necessarily things your character has collected. 250 words.

56

MACHINE IN THE GARDEN. Describe either a machine at least thirty years old or a very new machine. This could be a car engine, a DVD player with its cover removed, or a vacuum cleaner. The accurate description of this machine matters a great deal to the two characters who are trying to take it apart. They are *not* trying to fix it. Spend some time with the notion of how machines work. 500 words.

THINK OF YOUR FICTION as a small machine. If you took it apart, could you confidently rebuild it so it still worked? In "Shop Class as Soulcraft," in the *New Atlantis* (an online journal), Matthew B. Crawford describes how complex and inaccessible machines have become:

> Lift the hood on some cars now (especially German ones), and the engine appears a bit like the shimmering, featureless obelisk that so enthralled the cavemen in the opening scene of the movie *2001: A Space Odyssey*. Essentially, there is another hood under the hood. This creeping concealedness takes various forms. The fasteners holding small appliances together now often require esoteric screwdrivers not commonly available, apparently to prevent the curious or the angry from interrogating the innards. By way of contrast, older readers will recall that until recent decades, Sears catalogs included blown-up parts diagrams and conceptual schematics for all appliances and many other mechanical goods. It was simply taken for granted that such information would be demanded by the consumer.

---------------------------- 57)----------------------------

PHILOSOPHY AND ITS DISCONTENTS. Write one 450-word statement by a fictional character. This statement can be a self-defense (for a
crime or a misdeed) or a passionate support of someone or something.
Then write three 100-word critiques or rebuttals of this statement, written by three fictional characters who know this first character. This is all
you'll write. Let story leak in from around the edges of these four pieces
of prose. 750 words.

I'VE GONE TO A COUPLE OF PHILOSOPHY CONFERENCES in my life, and I've been
intrigued by how they work. A well-known philosopher gives a paper—
reading from an essay she has written. Often, two or three other philosophers deliver responses, which they've written in a week or two, since
receiving the paper by mail or e-mail. The rebuttals can be tough. They
tend to attack basic positions. Philosophers don't shy away from saying
to other philosophers, "You're dead wrong."

I attended a conference of ethical philosophers at Hampshire College
in Amherst, Massachusetts, once. This was the early 1980s and I was in
my mid-twenties, talking a lot about writing and storytelling whenever I
could. I had met both of the main speakers that day, a forty-five-year-old
woman who taught at the University of California, Berkeley, and a sixty-
year-old woman who taught at the University of Cambridge in England.
The conference was on abortion—attempts by the speakers to come to
ethical and logical terms over this thorny contemporary issue—and was
very unlike the analytic philosophy discussions I'd heard my father and
his colleagues indulge in over the years.

I asked both women why philosophers' stories were always, in my experience, so flat, using patently unrealistic characters and situations. Each woman had a different answer, but their talks that day told me much more. The elder of the two began the conference, discussing in abstract terms the problems of abortion and any moral or logical argument about it. She used a tale here and there as illustration, but the characters in her tales had funny names and did not act anything like plausible humans. Her thesis was intriguing, however, and I did not mind the silly stories as evidence because they did not interfere with her thoughtful argumentation.

The younger woman spoke next. My father, who was moderating the conference, had told me that ethical philosophy had lost its edge and cachet earlier in the century, but after the 1960s was making a comeback, and this Berkeley philosopher was one of its stars. She started her talk with a very concrete story about a husband and wife and male best friend of the husband climbing a mountain somewhere out West. I was drawn in. I knew how she was going to connect this to abortion, but knowing where the story was going did not dim my interest.

A man sat next to me in the audience. He'd been fidgeting the whole time, irritating me enough to make me think, from time to time, that I should move. The Berkeley philosopher got to the crux of her story. There was an accident, and the woman had a terrible choice: The three of them were in grave danger. Her husband, at the bottom of the three, was unlikely to survive. She could save herself and her husband's friend, but if she tried to save her husband or all three of them, all three of them would very probably die. Her husband told her so, and he told her to save herself and their friend. I was gripped by the story.

The man sitting next to me shot his hand up and shouted, "I have a question." My father looked perturbed. It was not normal or polite to interrupt a talk in its midst like this, but the Berkeley philosopher nodded tolerantly in the direction of this questioner. The man stood up, shaking. He said, "Well, it's not exactly a question. I was mountain-climbing with my wife and my best friend, and the exact same thing happened to us. I'm just stunned by your example." He went into some detail about the accident, in which his wife lost her life. The audience, the Berkeley philosopher, and my father were also stunned by this example. The moral of this story: Don't tell realistic stories in philosophy unless you know your audience very well.

LOVE & LUST

Christopher Lehmann-Haupt wrote of Elizabeth Hardwick in his obituary of her for the *New York Times*:

> Even while still at Columbia [University], Ms. Hardwick slipped into a Bohemian life—sharing a hotel apartment for a time with a young gay man, Greer Johnson; joining him in nightly searches for good jazz in the clubs on West Fifty-second Street, where she got to know, among others, Billie Holiday; scraping by on fellowships and family help—a life, as she later wrote in her semiautobiographical novel *Sleepless Nights*, signified by "love and alcohol and the clothes on the floor."

These three elements seem to play a recurring role in the activities of the lovelorn and loveless. I think of my own lonely single days, when every woman I met was a potential girlfriend or wife (not necessarily a lover), and I recall the odd unreality of actually succeeding occasionally, waking up next to a stranger, more or less, our clothes on the floor or at the foot of the bed. Sex for the first time between two people is a lot different than sex between two people who've been together ten or thirty years, but the difference is not huge. We are always strangers to each other when we engage in this most animal of acts. In the act of sex one often knows instantly whether this thing being established will last. How does one know? That's what you'll explore in these exercises.

---------------------------------- 58) ----------------------------------

SONG OF SONGS. Write a monologue addressed by one fictional character to her beloved. In this love poem in prose, the love being described
can be a metaphor for a larger issue (fame, power, good works), but it can
also simply be about an overwhelming love. The whole of this piece of
prose is an attempt to convince the recipient of it that he is truly loved. So
this is rhetoric, a sort of argument, except it's a method we're all pretty familiar with from love songs, plays, TV, and movies. As author of this love
poem in prose, try to see behind the curtains. Don't make the speaker
a fool, but she is besotted with love (or she is perhaps blind to some of
the more sketchy qualities of her loved one). You can certainly change the
genders or sexual orientation of these lovebirds. 750 words.

HERE ARE SOME FRAGMENTS from *Song of Songs* (which is also called *Song
of Solomon*):

> You have ravished my heart, my sister, my bride; you have ravished
> my heart with one of your glances, with one chain of your necklace.
> How fair is your love, my sister, my bride! How much better is your
> love than wine, and the smell of your ointment than all spices! ...
> Your navel is like a round goblet, which does not want liquor: Your
> belly is like a heap of wheat set about with lilies ... Your breasts are
> like young twin does ... Let us get up early to the vineyards; let us
> see if the vines flourish, whether the tender grapes appear, and the
> pomegranates bud forth: There will I give you my loves.

Here is what Carl Ernst has to say about *Song of Songs*:

In first-century Palestine the *Song of Songs* was sung in taverns. Yet in the Middle Ages, the love poetry of the text held a deep fascination for monks and nuns. This erotic masterpiece has always carried with it something more than merely a sensual attraction. Christian mystics used its language to express their longing for God. Monks in the Middle Ages made it the most copied book of the Bible.

It is intriguing that monks and nuns in the Middle Ages were so smitten by this poetry. Usually, descriptions of straightforward love are boring, mushy, or even pornographic. Spend some energy thinking about what it is about this loved one that really is unique and lovable. Beauty is important, but don't focus exclusively on appearances. Let us know that the writer of this prose love song sees into the soul of his beloved.

59

THE CARNAL & THE DOMESTIC. Write about sex as an ordinary, perhaps even laborious, activity—not an ecstatic event. Have your characters speak to each other as if they were not having sex (or plainly ask each other for help with the actual mechanics of the process of intercourse). Don't go overboard with this ho-hum attitude. They're still having sex and even enjoying it a good deal, but they may also have other things on their minds. 500 words.

LOOK AT WHAT DONALD ANTRIM DOES with sex in his first novel, *Elect Mr. Robinson for a Better World*:

> Hips rising, knees coming upward revealing the backs of Meredith's legs whitely imprinted with shapes of grass. I wriggled over, got

close and lay down beside her. I touched Meredith's stomach and her shoulder and her hair. I raised her lemonade glass, slipped ice into my mouth, held it melting against tongue and teeth before passing it between my wife's teeth, into her mouth, where, sucked by her, it dissolved.

"Ah," she said into my mouth.

"Ah," I breathed back.

"Ah."

"Ah."

"Yeah."

"Yeah."

"Hmn?"

"Yeah."

"How?"

"Slow."

"Mn."

"Ah."

"Mn."

"Oh."

"Easy."

"Sorry."

You might say this is cautious and even a little bit prudish in its descriptions. The actual talk is both accurate and withheld, but no picture of the sex really emerges. The two voices meld, so the male and female instructions or exclamations begin to resemble each other. What's lovely about this scenario is how moving the touching is. This is a couple that knows each other intimately, remembers past encounters and requests, and doesn't worry too much about errors or errant moves.

THE THREE STOOGES. Write about a man who falls in love with his ears—with what he hears his beloved say. He falls in love with a woman who falls in love with her eyes—with what she sees of her beloved. They briefly become a couple. They don't live together. Write a scene—a conversation, a night out, a walk—a week before they finally break up. Don't focus on the breakup, or the causes of the breakup. Instead give us a glimpse into this cracked, perhaps even broken, but also convivial and affectionate relationship. 750 words.

GRAYDON CARTER, THE EDITOR of *Vanity Fair*, says "Men like *The Three Stooges* movies, women don't; men fall in love with their eyes, women with their ears; men do not find it necessary to hold on to the neck of a straw, whereas women do." The first two categories are understandable. The third? I'm not sure what Carter is describing, although it sounds fairly sexual in its connotations.

SIDING WITH THE FATHER. Write a short fragment of fiction about an adolescent daughter (thirteen to fifteen years old) who sees too well into the intimacies of her parents' lives (because her parents' marriage is so broken both parents have confided to her way too much). She knows details of their complex and damaged sexual relationship, and she sides with her father. Let this daughter describe her parents' sex life in detail. The fragment of fiction should be about what she can know and what she can't possibly know. 500 words.

REBECCA TRAISTER REVIEWED Jane Fonda's memoir *My Life So Far* in the on-line journal *Salon*:

> [At the age of nine years old, Jane] Fonda remembers watching her mother try desperately to get her father's attention by walking around naked. "She was probably still very beautiful, but—oh, how I hate myself for this betrayal of her—I saw her through my father's judgmental eyes," writes Fonda. "She wasn't doing the right things to make him love her. And what it said to me was that unless you were perfect and very careful, it was not safe to be a woman. *Side with the man if you want to be a survivor.*"

From what I gather of messy divorces, the children often side with the parent who is in control, who has the power. In this exercise, focus on that power and on the slightly creepy intimacies children can be privy to when their parents have lost their typical parenting skills (if they ever had them).

62

BEAUTY & LUST. Write a short fragment of fiction in which two single people of the same sex are observing the same person of the opposite sex, with completely different readings of this person's attractiveness. Show us both points of view. Be direct about this. Woman A thinks this man is very attractive. Woman B thinks he is not. Do not follow through on this infatuation. Keep these two people in conversation with each other (and let us overhear their thoughts occasionally) about this object of their interests. This piece need not be realistic. Treat the situation the way a psychologist or an anthropologist might. As author, you are observing the divergence between two ways of seeing potential mates. This same person looks radically different to these two observers. Why? 750 words.

"WHY DOES LUST DEMAND BEAUTY?" the philosopher Alphonso Lingis asks. What is beauty? What is the purpose of a beautiful mate? David Von Drehle, in the *Washington Post*, talks about the relationship between beauty and human evolution:

> Stephen Marquardt, a reconstructive surgeon in Southern California who has made a career of studying beauty ... is one of a number of doctors and scientists probing the machinery that connects perceptions of beauty with human evolution. Beauty, they theorize, is the name we give to certain signals processed instinctively by our animal brains. It isn't invented by Hollywood or fashion magazines so much as it is programmed into our DNA ... [A] number of studies have shown that faces judged to be beautiful, regardless of culture, are highly symmetrical. Nature seems to have a bias in favor of balanced pairs—two arms, two legs, two eyes, two ears, two wings. Two recent studies found that greater symmetry in men corresponds with more and faster-swimming sperm. A Polish researcher named Grazyna Jasienska recently designed an experiment to determine whether symmetrical women have higher levels of the key reproductive hormone estradiol. In the journal *Evolution and Human Behavior*,

her team reports the results. They compared the left and right ring fingers of 183 Polish women between the ages of twenty-four and thirty-six. Women whose fingers differed in length by more than two millimeters formed the asymmetrical group. Their average estradiol levels were 13 percent lower than the symmetrical group average.

Marquardt indicates a kind of objective reality about beauty. Symmetry is obviously a desirable ideal, but there are all sorts of subjective ways we categorize beauty. In actors—especially very well-known actors—a flaw or set of flaws seems to make a famous beauty more intriguing to watch over time. The same may be true of day-to-day life.

63

LOVE & CHANCE. Write a very short scene in which two people meet by accident and fall madly in love. Meet by accident? They both reach for the same magazine in a bookstore; they are stuck in an elevator during a blackout; they're both robbed by the same mugger (though they are strangers) and go together to the nearby police station to identify the thief in a mug shot book. This should not only be about lust, although that should play some part in the story. These two characters fall in love and they'll stay in love—maybe not for a lifetime, but for a long time. Do this all in 500 words.

ALPHONSO LINGIS, THE AUTHOR OF *TRUST*, says, "Love is awakened only by chance. It flares up at the merest coincidence ... Nothing is more contrary to love than to exercise the reckoning mind so as to exclude adverse chances." Some couples ask, "What if we'd taken different light rail trains to the baseball game?" Few couples meet by accident, but all single people are on the lookout for accidental meetings.

—————————— 64)——————————

SYMBIOSIS. Write about a truly symbiotic relationship, which is healthy. Show us the reasons a couple is unusually interdependent—how, why, and at what levels. 750 words.

INTERDEPENDENCE, NESTING, AND SYMBIOSIS are all related. In the natural world, symbiosis is a close ecological relationship between the individuals of two different species. Don't write about a parasitic relationship. Among human beings, symbiosis is more metaphorical than a scientifically explainable phenomenon, like ants and acacia trees. Acacia ants defend their host trees and colony from mammals, lizards, snakes, and other insects, and the ants feed off secretions from the trees and take shelter among the thorns. These ants no longer have any other defense mechanisms than what the acacia tree offers.

All marriages are symbiotic and interdependent, to some degree. What would make a couple particularly dependent on each other? For example, a woman is very shy but good at friendship once she gets to know someone. Her husband is outgoing, funny, and good at attracting friends, but in the middle of friendships he loses confidence and gets selfish. He looks to his wife for guidance and advice.

—————————— 65)——————————

ADDICTED TO LOVE. Write a short piece of fiction in which the central character is addicted to love—but not necessarily addicted to sex. This character seeks a new conquest with some regularity not because she wants the experience of new lust, but because she wants to feel the early stages of love again. 750 words.

CYRIL CONNOLLY WROTE in his autobiography, *Enemies of Promise*, "All charming people must have something to conceal, usually their total dependence on the appreciation of others." The key to making this exercise work is to make this love addict charming and likeable, as well as damaged and reckless.

66

STRIPTEASE. Write a description of a striptease by a man or a woman for an audience of one other person. 500 words.

THE FRENCH LITERARY CRITIC and philosopher Roland Barthes compared the pleasures of narrative to those of the striptease in *The Pleasure of the Text*:

> Is not the most erotic portion of the body *where the garment gapes* [Barthes' emphasis]? ... it is intermittence ... which is erotic: the intermittence of skin flashing between two articles of clothing ... The pleasure of the text is not the pleasure of the corporeal striptease or of narrative suspense. In these cases, there is no tear, no edges: a gradual unveiling: The entire excitation takes refuge in the *hope* of seeing the sexual organ (schoolboy's dream) or in knowing the end of the story (novelistic satisfaction).

A tease like this in fiction is much harder to maintain. How does one keep a reader's eye on the clothing and the unveiling? There should be a reason for the reader to gaze at the process of disrobing, rather than skipping ahead to the naked body, although in fiction a naked body is just words. In film or on stage there are more concrete objects to behold.

Something to think about in this exercise is that fiction, though largely built on visual imagery, is not capable of drawing really detailed pictures in our minds. Fiction is often more like a sketch than an oil painting or a color photograph. We watch the action, not the still photos of the narrative.

— **67**)—

THE HOTEL BED. A twenty-five-year-old man and a forty-nine-year-old woman are in a hotel room. Both are sitting on the only bed, a king-sized bed, covers tossed around. They are fully clothed. Write a fragment of conversation between them. They are in this hotel room for their first sexual encounter, but the scene you're painting is what happens before that. 500 words.

DESPITE THE ARRIVAL on the contemporary scene of "cougars," forty- or fifty-something women who link up with twenty- or thirty-something men, this is still a startling idea for a set-piece scene. Older men and younger women are common and even a little boring, and that has been the subject of much fiction by men for many years. Explore the affection and attractions these two people have for each other, as well as the psychological reasons each is attracted to someone much younger or older.

— **68**)—

SERENDIPITY. Construct an elaborate two-person dance of engagement—a flirtation—that ends not in happiness and love and/or marriage but in dissolution. Do not write any scenes (of conversation and action). Write only summaries of the dates or encounters. Give us the overview of this brief relationship. The couple under the microscope has all the earmarks of a happy couple. They seem destined for each other. They have a great deal in common, but they also have useful differences (behaviors and quirks that nicely mirror each other's behaviors and quirks). But this couple does not stay together. Don't dwell on why they don't or can't last. Instead, focus on the simple fact that some people perfectly suited for each other don't make a good match. 750 words.

69

PILLOW TALK. Write a short fragment of prose in which you speak philosophically and in generalities about the rituals of courtship. Interrupt your musings with evidence—concrete examples of characters acting out common contemporary problems, as you see them, of this often-ridiculous process. Keep a nice balance of generalizations and specifics. 500 words.

I'VE ALWAYS LIKED THE MOVIE *PILLOW TALK*. Rock Hudson, Doris Day, and Perry Blackwell singing "Roly Poly" and "You Lied"; and Tony Randall saying, "You know Brad Allen, the Ex-Rex?" This is love as a pitched battle. A thirty-five-year-old woman who guards her chastity pretty carefully, but also lets Rock and Tony know that she knows a thing or two. Made in 1959, does the film mark the end of an era or the beginning of another one? It is an excellent example of the late screwball comedy, with lots of knowing conversation between the four major characters (Doris Day, Rock Hudson, Tony Randall, and Day's maid Thelma Ritter) about the pitfalls and pleasures of the mating game.

Almost a generation earlier, the character Barbara Stanwyck plays in the 1941 film *The Lady Eve* says, "A moonlit deck [of an ocean liner] is a woman's business office." This tough-girl stance is particular to *The Lady Eve*, but it also shows the harder edge of many of the great movies from that era. In his 1942 novel *Money in the Bank*, the incomparable P.G. Wodehouse describes a man who is surprised into a marriage proposal:

> He was still quite at a loss to understand how the ghastly thing had happened. The facts seemed to suggest that he must have let fall some passing remark which had given the girl the impression he was proposing to her, but he had no recollection of having done anything so cloth-headed. All he knew was that at a certain point of time at an evening party he had been a happy, buoyant young fellow, making light conversation to Myrtle Shoesmith behind a potted palm, and at another point of time, only a moment later, or so it seemed to him, he was listening appalled to Myrtle Shoesmith discussing cake and bridesmaids. The whole thing was absolutely sudden and unexpected, like an earthquake or a waterspout or any other Act of God.

In the 1930s and early 1940s, Hollywood's battle of the sexes was played on a level playing field. In the late 1950s, the field tipped toward chastity, even as the Hays Code loosened its grip on what could be described on-screen. Paradoxically these Doris Day movies became more prudish and yet much more directly about sex than any movie from the great era of screwball comedies could be (and perhaps why they were so entertaining—a sublimation of sexual energies).

70

DIVORCE SEX. Write a short scene about a divorced couple who have sex again, many years after their divorce. Get right to the point. Don't waste time telling us why they divorced, how acrimonious the process was, what the children experienced (if there were any). They're divorced and they find themselves in a situation that allows them to fall into bed together again. Explore the intimacy between these formerly intimate people. 500 words.

71

LOVE E-MAILS. Write a set of e-mails two people send professing their love to each other. You may need to include quite a few e-mails that are very brief, although you'll want at least a few that go on a bit longer. These two people have met in person, but they are much more comfortable speaking with each other by means of this medium. Why would that be? 750 words.

WHAT IS THE DIFFERENCE BETWEEN writing a letter and writing an e-mail? E-mails tend to be casual and more quickly composed. E-mails are notorious for enabling people to say things they wouldn't normally say out loud or on paper. The send button is so easy to press, and it is impossible to revoke an e-mail once sent. It takes a good deal more foresight and energy to print out (or handwrite) a letter, fold, seal, and stamp it, and then walk it over to the post office. But for these very reasons, e-mail might be an excellent medium for expressing infatuation slightly anonymously and with less repression. I have no experience whatsoever with text messaging, so I don't know how that medium would work for or against love letters.

THE MIND

Where does consciousness reside? Ancient Greek concepts of *thumos* (the nervous system), *phrenes* (lungs), *kradie* (heart, cardiac mind), *etor* (guts, belly), *noos* (perception, seeing), and *psyche* (the breath, life, soul eventually) were all once separate residences of consciousness (and some remain in speech to this day—heart and mind). Eventually (centuries of Greek civilization later) only two words remained to describe consciousness: *noos* and *psyche* (and they were relatively interchangeable).

Here is one farfetched but well-argued theory of the history of consciousness. Julian Jaynes, in his book *The Origin of Consciousness in the Breakdown of the Bicameral Mind*, argues that once we were two minds: the gods on one side (which rarely spoke or thought to us), the human self (but more or less an automaton) on other side (physiologically, it's true; the brain does have two parts, as much of the human body does—for spare parts). The modern conception of consciousness (an ego or self-consciousness) is a much later development than generally believed. Jaynes believes that humans until the seventh or eighth century B.C.E. were walking zombies, told by auditory hallucinations, under stress and in crucial situations, to act this way or that way (these voices were accepted as the gods speaking to them). Individual free will (the analog "I") developed in the centuries between *The Iliad* and *The Odyssey*, which Jaynes claims were written by at least two different people. Daniel Dennett says, "Jaynes has argued ... that [the brain's] capacities for self-exhortation and self-reminding are a prerequisite for the sorts of elaborated and long-term bouts of self-control without which agriculture, building projects, and other civilizing activities could not be organized."

Then there was a big jump: Descartes (the father of modern philosophy) separated mind and body. Descartes famously said, in Latin, *Cogito ergo sum* (I think therefore I am). It can be argued that our modern secular world grows out of this splitting off of mind and brain, mind and body, soul and self. How the modern mind works is one of the central fascinations of fiction.

72

THE INSISTENCE ON MEANING. Write an exercise in which an unnamed narrator attempts to make sense of everything he sees, connecting the dots in both logical and illogical ways, magical and realistic—or pseudo-realistic.

The world is not a rational place, full of meaning. We impose meaning on certain threads of the narrative we weave together in our daily lives, but we don't really expect everything to fit together logically and reasonably. A sinkhole doesn't open up in a bridge just after you've driven over it because you are safely past it. The sun doesn't come out from behind dark clouds just as you're about to propose marriage to your girlfriend. What you may want to do first, in this exercise, is write a 400-word scene that maps out the basic elements of this reality—a simple and undramatic set of moments and observations of the world. Then go back and add explanations of the cause and effect, although the explanations can and should be outrageous or simply nonsensical. 1,000 words.

IN THE FRANK BIDART POEM "The Arc," a character says, "I tell myself: 'Insanity is the insistence on meaning.'" This sounds counterintuitive, but if you think about it there is a great deal we encounter in our daily lives that is nonsense. If we tried to make sense of all the incongruous, even contradictory, events we face every hour, we'd go mad. If someone winks at us without a context, we don't know what it means. It might mean the person is attracted to us, that she is trying to communicate secretly, that she understands what we mean, or anything. As the context changes, the meaning of the wink changes. Meaning and context are constantly chang-ing, and our minds evolve just as often to input these changes.

73

BUZZING BLOOMING CONFUSION. Try to capture the true confu-sion of reality in a very short space. The exercise should have four layers. Layer One is numerical. Speak only of material things by the number of items—a block of sidewalk has six cracks; a shaft of sunlight has three sub-shafts. Layer Two works on the notion of sounds for objects that make no sound—this same section of sidewalk reverberates like a tuba no one is blowing into. Layer Three is just random sound effects, unat-tached to any concrete thing—twee-whit-tee-grack-grack-it. Layer Four is almost nothing but color—the blue slab of sidewalk purpled in the pink shaft of yellow light. Once you've got these four layers down, interleave them. 500 words.

Glenn C. Altschuler wrote in a review in the *Boston Globe* of Robert Richardson's biography, *William James: In the Maelstrom of American Modernism*, about this psychologist's explorations of his own mind (James did some of the pioneering studies of consciousness in the late nineteenth century):

> In a characteristically candid self-portrait, William James confessed that he raced around too much in a state of inner tension, preparing to engage and resist external stimuli: "left the present act inattentively done because I was preoccupied with the next act, failed to listen etc. because I was too eager to speak, kept up when I ought to have kept down, been jerky, angular, rapid, precipitate, let my mind run ahead of my body etc. etc." Despite—or because of—this "buzzing blooming confusion," James, that "adorable genius," made dazzling contributions to psychology, philosophy, and the study of religion.

74

INFORMATION SICKNESS. Write a fragment of an interior monologue by a beleaguered human being who is doing four things at once—managing two of them quite well, perhaps the third or fourth things not so well. It might be difficult to make this intriguing if all four activities are on a computer or a cell phone, because the description of this operation resists reality. By its very nature, online existence is virtual reality. The *Oxford English Dictionary* defines the word *virtual* (as it applies to computers) as "not physically existing as such but made by software to appear to do so from the point of view of the program or the user." So try to make the simultaneous operations concrete and capable of generating some kind of interesting meaning. 500 words.

THOMAS L. FRIEDMAN, IN THE *NEW YORK TIMES*, November 1, 2006, said:

> Linda Stone, the technologist ... [who] labeled the disease of the Internet age "continuous partial attention"—two people doing six things, devoting only partial attention to each one— ... remarked: "We're so accessible, we're inaccessible. We can't find the off switch on our devices or on ourselves ... We want to wear an iPod as much to listen to our own playlists as to block out the rest of the world and protect ourselves from all that noise. We are everywhere—except where we actually are physically."

In his novel *Easy Travel to Other Planets*, which was published long before the Internet, Ted Mooney imagined something he called Information Sickness. Other writers since then have explored the notion, including Don DeLillo and Douglas Coupland. *Encyclopedia Neurotica* by Jon Winokur (there really is such a book) dryly defines the syndrome: "Anxiety produced by information overload, especially from TV newscasts, with their guiding programming principle, 'if it bleeds, it leads.' Symptoms can include sleep disturbance, substance abuse, and *compassion fatigue*." The italics at the end seem to be both a reference to another entry in the encyclopedia and a weary exclamation. We are swallowing (but not digesting) too much information. The younger you are, the more gadgets you probably have and the more hooked up to your friends you are. Is this a good thing? Are we gaining anything from our umbilical connection to the world by means of PDAs, cell phones, the Internet, iPods?

—————————————————————(**75**)—————————————————————

ON HASHISH. Write a storylet from the point of view of a character who has taken a mild drug like marijuana (or at least a milder type of the plant). 500 words.

THE PHILOSOPHER WALTER BENJAMIN and several other intellectual friends took various drugs for scientific experiments in the 1920s and 1930s. In December 1927, Benjamin noted his first impressions of the experience:

> Boundless goodwill. Falling away of neurotic-obsessive anxiety complexes. The sphere of "character" opens up. All those present take on hues of the comic. At the same time, one steeps oneself in their aura. Poetic evidence in the phonetic: At one point I maintain that, in answer to a question a little earlier, I had used the expression "for a long time" purely as a result (so to speak) of my perception of a long time in the sounding of the words of the question and answer. I experience this as poetic evidence. One is very much struck by how long one's sentences are. This, too, connected with horizontal extension and (probably) with laughter. Aversion to information. Rudiments of a state of rapture. Great sensitivity to open doors, loud talk, music. Reluctant (and slow) to follow the thoughts of others.

I do not advocate the taking of drugs, although, in the interest of full disclosure (as journalists say), I have smoked hashish and marijuana hundreds of times (but very little for the last twenty years because of blood sugar imbalances); inhaled cocaine four or five times in my twenties;

taken acid twice, also in my twenties; eaten mushrooms a couple of times; and tried peyote once. I started to dream up and write the exercises for *The 3 A.M. Epiphany* when I first began teaching because I grew tired of my undergraduates trying to describe the ecstatic experience of some form of artificial derangement. Students did not work terribly hard at describing the state of alienation, expecting their audiences to recognize the markers of being "high" without the effort of detailing what this experience was.

You might also pick up Henri Michaux's *The Major Ordeals of the Mind and the Countless Minor Ones*, which is a book-length treatise on the subject of drug-taking and disorientation. Michaux was a poet, artist, and travel writer, but this book is a wonderfully deadpan scientific study from the mind of a poet.

―――――――――――――― **76**)――――――――――――――

LEARNING TO SEE. Imagine a person blind for many years (but not born blind) who has just regained her sight. This will not be an easy process to describe, but try to show us the completely chaotic patterns of the world this person "sees" but cannot and will not ever be able to understand. 500 words.

OLIVER SACKS DESCRIBES an argument between two philosophers in the eighteenth century over this question: "If a person born blind were able to recognize a globe or a cube by touch and was then given sight, could he recognize it by sight?" The answer turned out to be no. This person "saw" everything, "but he could recognize nothing; nothing had meaning for him. People in this state may be able to draw perfectly accurately, they may be able to copy or reproduce, but they may not know what they are copying or reproducing."

In *The Book of the Mind*, by Stephen Wilson, Sacks gets at the basics of the way the mind works:

> There is no little man, there is no homunculus in the brain looking at the world, there is something like fifty visual systems, all contributing, all playing their own tune, all talking to one another, and their orchestration yields the apparently seamless visual world—my visual world, your visual world ... All you know is that you see the world. To you it seems seamless; the mechanisms that are involved in this wonderful synthesis or integration are completely inaccessible to introspection.

Keep this in mind as you explore your character's method of reintegrating this basic sense back into her mental machinery.

77

BLIND. Write a short scene from a third-person attached point of view of a character that has very recently lost his sight. Do not tell us how this person became blind. 500 words.

A PERSON BLIND FROM BIRTH has developed his other senses—smell, touch, hearing. Would someone who's just lost his sight have the same overdeveloped senses? The obvious emotion to explore in this situation would be terror, but don't depend too much on that emotion. Curiosity could also be explored. Close your eyes (or wear a snug-fitting blindfold) for an hour and get a sense of what you'd feel of your surroundings.

— 78)—

MULTILINGUAL. Write a short fragment of fiction from the point of view (and in the voice of) a truly multilingual person who is listening to two different languages spoken by a group of people. This narrator of yours is at the center of this group, not necessarily the translator, but he takes on that role from time to time. Someone speaking in one of these languages your narrator understands is lying about something crucial to this group of people. If you have no idea what it would be like to understand perfectly at least two different languages, guess. The appeal of a character like this, for a fiction writer, might be the insights he has into several cultures at once—a kind of limited omniscience. 750 words.

GEORGE STEINER, IN HIS ESSAY "EXTRATERRITORIAL," talks about the early nineteenth-century German Jewish poet Heinrich Heine:

> The language of Shakespeare, of Montaigne, of Luther, embodies an extreme local strength, an assertion of specific, "untranslatable" identity. For the writer to become bi- or multilingual in the modern way, genuine shifts of sensibility and personal status had to occur. These are visible, for the first time perhaps, in Heine. Binary values characterize his life. He was a Jew with a Christian upbringing and a Voltairean view of both traditions. His poetry modulates continually between a romantic-conservative and a radical, satiric stress. Politics and personal mood made him a commuter in Europe. This condition determined his equal currency in French and in German and gave his German poetry a particular

genius. "The fluency and clarity which Heine appropriated from current speech," says T.W. Adorno, "is the very opposite of native 'at-homeness.' Only he who is not truly at home inside a language uses it as an instrument."

Steiner's argument is that the multilingual mind seems capable of a wider range of thinking—almost schizophrenic in its bouncing back and forth between poles. His essay examines a handful of modern bilingual writers—Nabokov, Beckett, and Kafka—whom he calls extraterritorials. These are, he claims, crucial to twentieth-century thinking. More than half the world speaks at least two languages. Only one in seven Americans speaks more than one language. People who speak more than one language do not suffer from brain overload. When you write about a language other than English, you do not need to use that language. Just say, "In Arabic she said she didn't drink alcohol."

79

AUTISM. Write from the point of view of a ten-year-old who suffers from this disease of extreme aloneness. If you know nothing about autism, do some research. Or simply dive into the experience and try to imagine a person so cut off from the rest of humanity. I hope you'll be interested in how this child's mind works rather than how the outside world sees the body in which this mind is housed. 750 words.

DAVID COHEN WRITES ABOUT AUTISM in the *Chronicle of Higher Education*:

Childhood autism was first described in 1943 by Leo Kanner, a child psychiatrist at the Johns Hopkins University, who spent five years studying eleven children possessed with an "extreme aloneness from the beginning of life." He borrowed the word "autism," derived from the Greek *autos,* meaning "self," from the Swiss researcher Eugen Bleuler ... No two young autists are the same. Some will manage to lead relatively ordinary, even intellectually exceptional, lives, while others may need to be institutionalized ... Among the behaviors most linked to the disorder are poor language and social skills, and a propensity for repetitive, frequently obsessional behavior, including hand-flapping, toe-walking, and self-injury. Autistic kids will often repeat the same words or phrases over and over, or immerse themselves in weirdly narrow interests, spinning to the sound of a rock album until they drop or else, perhaps, staring at a leaf on a tree until the sun goes down.

Read Eli Gottlieb's *The Boy Who Went Away* for a searing perspective on being the only sibling of a severely autistic brother.

— **80**)—

NARCISSISM. Spend some time writing a piece of incomplete fiction about a narcissist. Briefly, this is someone who is preoccupied with fantasies of success, power, brilliance, beauty, or ideal love. Narcissists lack empathy and are unwilling to recognize or identify with the feelings and needs of others. This sort of character can be quite annoying, but try to love this person, even if the character does quite a bit that you find repugnant. 500 words.

HERE IS A SIMPLE DESCRIPTION of the disorder from Internet Mental Health (www.mentalhealth.com):

Narcissistic personality disorder is a condition characterized by an inflated sense of self-importance, need for admiration, extreme self-involvement, and lack of empathy for others. Individuals with this disorder are usually arrogantly self-assured and confident. They expect to be noticed as superior. Many highly successful individuals might be considered narcissistic. However, this disorder is only diagnosed when these behaviors become persistent and very disabling or distressing ... Vulnerability in self-esteem makes individuals with this disorder very sensitive to criticism or defeat. Although they may not show it outwardly, criticism may haunt these individuals and may leave them feeling humiliated, degraded, hollow, and empty. They may react with disdain, rage, or defiant counterattack. Their social life is often impaired due to problems derived from entitlement, the need for admiration, and the relative disregard for the sensitivities of others.

81

DRIVING. Write a fragment of fiction that takes place in a car. The driver is a novice—maybe not driving for the first time but still very early in her experience of automobiles. Pay special attention to the process of driving itself, as well as its subsidiary activities. The driver is being distracted by one or more passengers. Try to present the visual information one receives in a novel way—show us the succession of images out the windshield and the side and rear windows. The idea of this exercise is to get you to play with the notion of distraction and multitasking, especially at an age when this one kind of multitasking is not second nature. 500 words.

How we command our brains to do all the various actions that make up driving is just one example of the sort of mental activity that goes on below the surface of consciousness. In this exercise, explore the way the mind operates occasionally on autopilot, so to speak. Here is how Verlyn Klinkenborg describes driving for the first time, from the *New York Times*:

> That first time behind the wheel, probably in 1965, I could feel myself manipulating the machine through an unimaginable series of linkages with a clumsy device called the steering wheel. The car—a Dodge from the late 1950s, without power steering—felt more like a fallout shelter than something mobile. I had very little sense of where it began or ended. I was keenly aware of what it prevented me from seeing. A highway was just a linear succession of blind spots. As for backing up, how could you really trust what the mirrors told you unless you got out and checked? The transmission—manual, of course—was an instrument of betrayal. To drive down the road, those first few times, was to lurch through a series of unrelated states of being.

For another example of how to show a "succession of images out the windshield and the side and rear windows," look at Vladimir Nabokov's autobiography *Speak, Memory* on the subject of views out a moving train:

> The door of the compartment was open and I could see the corridor window [of the train], where wires—six thin black wires—were doing their best to slant up, to ascend skywards, despite the lightning blows dealt them by one telegraph pole after another; but just

as all six, in a triumphant swoop of pathetic elation, were about to reach the top of the window, a particularly vicious blow would bring them down, as low as they had ever been, and they would have to start all over again.

—————————————— 82)——————————————

NUMERICAL COGNITION. Write a fragment of fiction about someone who keeps finding two consecutive numbers all around her. She has to work sometimes to find these numbers—but they are very obvious other times. This character's occupation has very little to do with math or numbers. Is this person going mad? Has she suffered brain damage without knowing it? Is the world simply aligned in a way that causes two numbers to recur in unusual places? 750 words.

JIM HOLT, IN THE *NEW YORKER*, March 3, 2008:

One morning in September, 1989, a former sales representative in his mid-forties entered an examination room with Stanislas Dehaene, a young neuroscientist based in Paris. Three years earlier, the man, whom researchers came to refer to as Mr. N, had sustained a brain hemorrhage that left him with an enormous lesion in the rear half of his left hemisphere. He suffered from severe handicaps: His right arm was in a sling; he couldn't read; and his speech was painfully slow. He had once been married, with two daughters, but was now incapable of leading an independent life and lived with his elderly parents. Dehaene had been invited to see him because his impairments included severe acalculia, a general term for any one of several deficits in number processing. When asked to add 2 and 2, he answered "three." He could still count and recite a sequence like 2, 4, 6, 8, but he was incapable of counting downward from 9, differentiating odd and even numbers, or recognizing the numeral 5 when it was flashed in front of him.

To Dehaene, these impairments were less interesting than the fragmentary capabilities Mr. N had managed to retain. When he was shown the numeral 5 for a few seconds, he knew it was a numeral rather than a letter and, by counting up from 1 until he got to the right integer, he eventually identified it as a 5. He did the same thing when asked the age of his seven-year-old daughter. In the 1997 book *The Number Sense*, Dehaene wrote, "He appears to know right from the start what quantities he wishes to express, but reciting the number series seems to be his only means of retrieving the corresponding word."

When you've finished a draft of this exercise, count up the number of words and the number of sentences. Revise the piece to include these two numbers somehow. If the numbers are six and seven, for instance, make a list of six-letter and seven-letter words and throw a few more of them into the narrative. Scatter throughout the fragment six-word and seven-word sentences, back-to-back. Why do this? You are studying a very specific, even unrealistic form of derangement (despite what Stanislas Dehaene has discovered), but this character will also have to have a life she's living. Whatever these numbers end up meaning, you may find you are writing a good piece of fiction that has nothing to do with these numbers.

EMOTION

I wrote extensively about emotion in the section of exercises Thought and Emotion in *The 3 A.M. Epiphany*. Let me quote one small part of that introduction: "The primary building block of fiction is emotion, and it's intriguing that the very word contains this idea of movement. Characters are convincing and plausible only by the way they move from one state of mind to another, from one crisis to another. We are *moved* by fiction that represents emotion faithfully and accurately."

─────────────── **83** ───────────────

PAIN. Write a fragment of fiction about excruciating pain a character is experiencing. The pain, however, has nothing to do with the story the character is telling. It would be a very good idea to do some research on pain. Do a lot of research. At the same time, this is a fragment of a story in which the main character is struggling to observe the world and his intimates (or strangers) while ignoring some kind of gnawing, throbbing feeling—a migraine, a badly swollen sprained ankle, a ruptured appendix. 500 words.

WHY DO I HAVE YOU DO this sort of thing all the time? Why should writers write about a sky full of attacking flying saucers without having the characters look up at this sky full of menace? Writing about any sensation is a little like the experience of trying to describe pain. Doctors know how difficult it is for patients to depict pain, or doctors should know this, and rarely seriously investigate descriptions of pain. But more than showing us how a character experiences pain without articulating it to anyone else, I want you to write about a character handicapped by something. Most fiction about human beings takes for granted the clarity of their sensory perceptions of the world. But we also know that most people are at best distracted, and at worst hobbled, by emotional or physical pain.

Paula Kamen, in an article in the *New York Times*, February 12, 2008, speaks of the way migraines might have affected the character of Lewis Carroll's wonderland:

> When he plunged Alice down the rabbit hole, the author Lewis Carroll was armed with a powerful tool from his own inner life to make his heroine's journey all the weirder: migraines. He certainly took advantage of the vision distortions that accompanied his particular spells to make Alice feel as clumsy and disoriented as possible in her far-from-wonderful "wonderland." The malady also appears specifically throughout the story as directly afflicting other characters, such as Tweedledee, who comments, "Generally I am very brave ... only today I happen to have a headache."

--------------------(**84**)--------------------

HIDING EMOTIONS. Write about two people speaking to each other. They both hide their deepest emotions but act on them helplessly anyway. 500 words.

TASHA ROBINSON, IN THE *ONION*, says, "*Dune* still feels like a David Lynch film. He's always had a masterful grasp on the way people hide their deepest emotions but helplessly act on them anyway, and the way crisis heightens such emotions' repression and expression."

—————————————————— **85**) ——————————————————

REDNESS. Write a short piece of fiction that depends on a character's precise perception of or reaction to the color red. Red could make this character very happy, very sad, angry, giggly, or catatonic. Red could be the solution to a problem this character has been pondering for many months. 500 words.

NATALIE ANGIER, IN THE *NEW YORK TIMES*, February 5, 2007, noted:

> Human eyes, like those of other great apes, seem to be all-around fabulous fruit-finding devices, for they are more richly endowed with the two cone types set to red and yellow wavelengths than with those sensitive to short, blue-tinged light. That cone apportionment allows us to discriminate among subtle differences in fruit ruddiness and hence readiness, and may also explain why I have at least forty lipsticks that I never wear compared with only three blue eye shadows.

Bulls are supposed to get mad at the color red. Humans in a room painted red are more prone to anger. When I was eight years old, I woke up in my cousin's bedroom in the middle of the night. Tom's walls were painted a brilliant, almost frightening red. When I woke up I saw the head of the devil—bright red, with horns and flashing red eyes, staring in at me from this first-floor bedroom window. My family was staying across town in a borrowed home—my father was teaching at the University of Minnesota for the summer. None of this felt familiar to me, especially the devil's head in my cousin's bedroom window. I quietly left his room and awoke my aunt and asked her politely if she could drive me back to the house my parents and siblings were staying at. I don't remember if she did. I don't think I told her about the devil in the window.

— 86)—

GRIEF. Write a short monologue by a person who is openly and deeply grieving over the death of a friend or loved one. Do not make this grief the only subject of this little monologue (but you should certainly mention the death). The central action of the "story" should be fairly ordinary, even banal, and come weeks after the death of this friend or loved one. 750 words.

EMERSON SAID, "I GRIEVE that I cannot grieve." By this he may have meant that grief is a mysterious and unpredictable process. This exercise is not among the group that concerns death because this piece should not be about death, but about the emotion of lamentation. Perhaps we grieve in order to assert the fact that we are still living. We mourn the dead (or we even keen for them) to admit our guilt at surviving, as much as to communicate our sense of the absence of this person.

— 87)—

ENJOY THE PROCESS. Write a very short story in which the main character is happy, following some of Gretchen Rubin's rules below, but silently, without pronouncing any of them aloud (and without using the name Gretchen, although it is a lovely and archaic name). 750 words.

HERE ARE GRETCHEN RUBIN'S TWELVE COMMANDMENTS for her Happiness Project (www.happiness-project.com/happiness_project/):

1. Be Gretchen. 2. Let it go. 3. Act as I would feel. 4. Do it now. 5. Be polite and be fair. 6. Enjoy the process. 7. Spend out. 8. Identify the problem. 9. Lighten up. 10. Do what ought to be done. 11. No calculation. 12. There is only love.

You'll have to decide if you want us to observe a happy person from outside or watch her happiness from within. Patricia Cohen, in her *New York Times* review of David Michaelis's biography of Charles Schulz, *Schulz and Peanuts*, describes the sadness that seemed necessary for Schulz's art and why much of his happy second marriage did not get much airplay in the biography:

> "David [Michaelis] couldn't put everything in," [Jean Schulz, Charles Schulz's second wife] said, but added, "I think Sparky's melancholy and his dysfunctional first marriage are more interesting to talk about than twenty-five years of happiness." She quoted her husband's frequent response to why Charlie Brown never got to kick the football: "Happiness is not funny."

But happiness can be much more complex than it is given credit for being. Writers have been taught in American fiction workshops to look for conflict and crisis, and many inexperienced writers therefore seek out dysfunction and unhappiness, thinking they are necessarily linked to those crucial aspects of a good "story." But we can make happiness and functionality a much more interesting part of our narratives. In any case, a lot of contemporary American fiction seems to condescend toward its dysfunctional subject matter. If you do choose to write about how your characters regularly and ritually fail in life and love, be fair to them. Allow yourself a few kindnesses and moments of redemption, even in the midst of a long arc of decline and error.

—————————————— **88**)———————————————

LAUGHTER IS HOW WE CONNECT. Write a short scene in which several friends are unable to stop laughing. This shouldn't be like an episode of hiccups, an unstoppable and even frightening thing. These people are genuinely laughing, in that phase of an evening in which everything is funny. Explore the friendships between bursts of laughter. How do you describe different types of laugh? *Tee-hee-hee-ankh*. Or you could simply say, "More general laughter ensued." 500 words.

STEVEN JOHNSON, IN *DISCOVER MAGAZINE*, quotes scientist Robert Provine on laughter:

> "You're thirty times more likely to laugh when you're with other people than you are when you're alone—if you don't count simulated social environments like laugh tracks on television"... Think how rarely you'll laugh out loud at a funny passage in a book but how quick you'll be to give a friendly laugh when greeting an old acquaintance. Laughing is not an instinctive physical response to humor, the way a flinch is a response to pain or a shiver to cold. Humor is crafted to exploit a form of instinctive social bonding.

Portraying laughter in a piece of fiction is very hard. Even more difficult is to present a funny situation without, in a sense, pausing to examine it, as the writer. Stand-up comedians learn to wait out laughter. Writers have no such difficulty, except when they try to make us observe laughter.

In 1985, I gave a public reading of a story I'd been working on up to the morning of the reading. I did not think it was a very good story, let alone funny. I'd never thought of myself as a humorist. When I read the story, the audience made a strange group noise toward the beginning of the reading. I honestly did not know what the sound was for an instant, until I realized it was laughter. As I read, I got used to the laughing, although I did not know when to expect it. The story was about my family driving through Russia in 1969, and I thought it was a sharp, serious, even mournful examination of our dysfunction and difficulties, as well as a realistic portrait of that odd trip. But later I saw that it was a funny story.

—————————————— **89**)——————————————

SOBBING. In "Thirteen Writing Prompts" from *McSweeney's* online (www. mcsweeneys.net/2006/5/4wiencek.html), Dan Wiencek proposes this tart and explosive exercise: "Write a short scene in which one character reduces another to uncontrollable sobs without touching him or speaking." Take this instruction seriously. The person who causes the other person to sob does not cry or react at all to the sobbing person. 500 words.

THE EXERCISES DAN WIENCEK has composed are very funny, and some are very useful (which doesn't always seem to be his intent). He mainly wants to satirize a process I've obviously been intrigued by for a long time. But this one exercise is surprising. What could explain the ability of someone to reduce someone else to sobbing? We know people who can elicit laughter by simply walking into a room or arching an eyebrow. What happens when this other reflex is triggered?

―――――――――――――― **90** ――――――――――――――

THE COLLECTOR OF INJUSTICES. Write from the point of view some-one in authority—a guidance counselor, a cop, a school vice-principal—who tells us of several encounters with a collector of injustices (see below). This observer may be sympathetic, but he may also be a little frightened or at least put off by this person. 750 words.

IN THE *WASHINGTON POST*, August 10, 2007, Jerry Markon speaks about the Virginia Tech killer:

> Investigators said they are pursuing a number of possible theories to explain [the Virginia Tech mass murderer Seung-Hui] Cho's actions but still lack the evidence to settle on one particular explanation. They declined to comment on a possible theory federal agents un-veiled in June, which suggested that Cho displayed many of the same characteristics of a criminal behavioral profile called the "Collector of Injustice," or someone who considers any misfortune against him the fault or responsibility of others.

―――――――――――――― **91** ――――――――――――――

SELECTIVE MUTISM. Write a short fragment of fiction with a limited omniscient narration about a person who could be suffering from this dis-order (see below). Do not make this person a potential murderer or even dangerous or frightening. She is simply unable or unwilling to interact with other human beings the vast majority of the time. Work on evoking this notion somehow, without pressing the character to speak. Let us see how others view the character, but don't go inside their minds. Don't invade this character's thoughts—in fact, never show us the thoughts of this character, only the actions and gestures. Omniscient narration, in this case, might be a useful tactic for expressing the mute character's approach to the world and to people. 500 words.

BRIGID SCHULTE AND TIM CRAIG, in the *Washington Post*, August 27, 2007, also speak about the social behavior of the Virginia Tech murderer, Seung-Hui Cho:

> Fairfax County school officials determined that Seung-Hui Cho suffered from an anxiety disorder so severe that they put him in special education and devised a plan to help, according to sources familiar with his history, but Virginia Tech was never told of the problem. The disorder made Cho unable to speak in social settings and was deemed an emotional disability, the sources said. When he stopped getting the help that Fairfax was providing, Cho became even more isolated and suffered severe ridicule during his four years at Virginia Tech, experts suggested. In his senior year, Cho killed thirty-two students and faculty members and himself in the deadliest shooting by an individual in U.S. history. The condition, called selective mutism, is a symptom of a larger social anxiety disorder. It prompted the Fairfax school system to develop a detailed special education plan to help ease Cho's fears so he might begin to talk more openly, the sources said. Part of his individualized program in Fairfax ex-

cused Cho from participating in class discussions, according to the sources, who spoke on condition of anonymity because of the confidentiality of Cho's records. Another part of the plan called for private therapy to resolve his underlying anxiety. The therapy and special provisions were "apparently effective," the sources said.

We tend to pay attention to disorders like this one when a person suffering from it does something awful and newsworthy. In this exercise, I hope you'll be more interested in the problem of creating a character who can navigate the world without speaking to people.

92

WE THINK WITH THE OBJECTS WE LOVE. Think of the one object you own that means more than anything else of all your objects. Maybe first, it would be good to list five of these objects, then ponder each one for a while until one of them stands out clearly as the most important or evocative. Write a long paragraph about this object—its history, its utility, its shape and color and scent. Put that paragraph aside for a week. When you look at the paragraph again, read it several times. Immediately write a piece of narrative about this object. Write this narrative as if someone else other than you owned and cherished the object. 500 words.

IN *EVOCATIVE OBJECTS: THINGS WE THINK WITH*, Sherry Turkle says, "Objects bring philosophy down to earth. We think with the objects we love; we love the objects we think with." In the Canadian newspaper the *National Post*, Robert Fulford describes one person Turkle wrote about in *Evocative Objects*:

[Archeologist] David Mitten focused on a five-thousand-year-old limestone axe head that turned up a few generations ago on his grandfather's Ohio farm. He keeps it on his fireplace mantel partly because learning in detail about how it must have been made told him about the patience and industry of the civilization that produced it. He knows that someone hunted for a stone of the right size and then began turning it into an axe head by "seemingly endless pecking, pounding, chipping, and grinding," probably over several years. That produced its sharp edge and the grooves for attaching it to a wooden handle. The handle was split at one end, softened in water, then slowly bent around the head's grooves. Wet rawhide was tied around the ends; when dried, it shrank, binding itself to the stone. The maker, Mitten argues, freed this axe head from the stone in which it was encased—as Michelangelo, millennia later, said he freed the human forms buried within his blocks of marble. Pondering the axe head sent Mitten toward his career as an archeologist of ancient cultures. "I owe it a great deal."

93

A CURSE. Write a curse. This curse is being written by one character against another character. Use characters you have already written about for this exercise. A curse is a malevolent appeal to a supernatural being for harm to come to somebody. The character making this malevolent appeal should be known to us only by what he writes. We will get to know the character being cursed a good deal better than the person doing the cursing. Older versions of curses involved making effigies of the victim. Keep that in mind as you work up this curse. Behind the curse is a great deal of anger, even hatred. It might be wonderful if your curse is imaginative, strange, even funny, but don't lose sight of the fact that the curse also hopes for serious harm to come to this character. 500 words.

DEATH

The United States is obsessed with death—murdertainment, slasher films, documentaries about serial killers, horror movies, and video games that allow the player to kill dozens of characters. Periodically, mass murderers appear in shopping malls, college classrooms, on airplanes. We are both sensitized and desensitized to the trauma of death. But we are also still quite uncomfortable talking about death. Think of all the euphemisms for it—pass away, kick the bucket, meet your maker, expire. In 1995, I taught a then relatively unknown book, *The Talented Mr. Ripley* by Patricia Highsmith, to a class of mine. The book follows the story of Ripley and it subverts the plot of an earlier novel, Henry James's *The Ambassadors*. Ripley kills several characters in the novel and gets away, at the end, scot-free and apparently guiltless. Highsmith wrote four more Ripley novels, perfecting his amoral, clever, but always murderous persona. My students were horrified to discover they sympathized with this character that got away with murder.

My point is that this kind of amoral investigation of the murderer and the psychotic subject has grown more common and more prominent in the last decade. Tony Soprano and Dexter are two examples of this fascination with high-functioning psychopaths. Around the time of the psychopathic Roman emperor Nero (37–68 A.C.E.), so many condemned men were being put to death each week in ancient Rome that they were brought to the theater and, when a character was to die on stage, the condemned man was brought in to replace the actor and actually put to death on stage. Have we entered a moment in history like decadent Rome?

In my first stories, I often killed off characters because I didn't know what to do with them. I see something like this in my undergraduates' fiction. There is also a fascination with death. In these exercises I aim to turn young writers away from the easy use of death. A typical gunshot wound won't kill someone immediately, despite what you see in the movies. A shooting victim dies slowly, painfully, without dignity. Death is messy, and most murders are committed for banal and stupid reasons. Calvin Trillin's deadpan book *Killings* explores sixteen murders that weren't big news. A young man who has been shot by his best friend says, moments before he dies, "You shot me, you rat." Trillin notices how ordinary and usual most murders are, how surprisingly they conform to the rest of our lives—how much they resemble normal behavior except for the fact that murder is not acceptable or normal.

Brian Evenson, in his story "Altmann's Tongue," listens in on a murderer's thoughts after the character has killed two people (the first, he thinks, justifiably, the second unjustifiably):

It had been right to kill Altmann, I thought. Given the choice to kill or not to kill Altmann, I had chosen the former and had, in fact, made the correct choice. We go through life at every moment making choices. There are people, Altmann among them, who, when you have sent a bullet through their skull, you know you have done the right thing. It is people like Altmann who make the rest of it worthwhile, I thought, while people like Horst, when killed, confuse life further. The world is populated by Altmanns and Horsts, the former of which one should riddle with bullets on the first possible occasion, the latter of which one should perhaps kill, perhaps not: Who can say?

Perhaps only Brian Evenson (or Quentin Tarantino) could get away with this kind of philosophizing in the face of depraved behavior. Don't try this at home.

94

OBITUARY. Write a story that mimics the form of an obituary, but try to make it a funny obituary, like this one, for Davis Mortimer (not his real name) in the *Daily Hampshire Gazette* (the Northampton, Massachusetts newspaper) in late 2006:

> With trumpets blaring, Zeus, god of gods, called Davis Mortimer to His Heavenly Pantheon on November 21, 2006. He (Mortimer, not Zeus) was the second white child born in the new maternity ward at Cooley Dickinson Hospital in Northampton on his father's birth-

day, July 2, 1930. His mother Helen (Hancock) needed all the help she could get. Mortimer was reared on a small farm in Worthington. Sickly as a child, his parents often contemplated drowning him in Watt's Brook that flowed (trickled in the summer) behind the house into which (the brook, not the house) they deposited other trash, sewage, and cow manure. After being partially educated at local schools, Mortimer matriculated in the class of 1952 at the University of Massachusetts, formerly Mass Aggie. Here he failed to distinguish himself in any meaningful way, and managed to alienate a number of his classmates and professors. Upon graduation without honors, Mortimer was drafted into the Army and served in Korea before and after the armistice. There he learned more than at college—never volunteer, be cowardly to survive, don't circulate petitions, and keep away from indigenous females. Returning home ill prepared for an occupation, he was strangely accepted by the University of Michigan Graduate School where he tried to prepare for an acceptable if not respectable occupation. A thirty-five-year career as a museum and historical agency director followed. He moved from state to state five times to keep ahead of his reputation. He completed his career ignominiously in Cooperstown in 1992. On his demise, he was a member of no organization, club, or charity.

Who writes an obituary, usually? Not the person who's died, in the vast majority of cases. Famous people who are aging often have an obituary on ice, as it were, ready for the moment when they die. Davis Mortimer's obit sounds like it was written by him, as he was dying, or perhaps long before he died.

A short story that begins with an obituary might seem to need to be about that person. It doesn't have to be about that person. 500 words.

—————————————— **95**)——————————————

IMAGINE YOUR OWN DEATH. This is a tough one. It would be very easy to get maudlin or perhaps even vengeful on this subject. *None of you knew how much you'd miss me.* But an actual scenario with your own possible death in it might be sobering and very weird to write—something to challenge your own notions of the romanticism of death. Use your own name. Don't be dramatic. Let yourself yield voluptuously to this strange experience. This is perhaps the purest fiction you can write. You should also be prepared to freak out over this exercise, if you take it seriously. 500 words.

HERE IS A NARRATIVE OF THE IMPROMPTU CREMATION of the early nineteenth-century British Romantic poet Percy Shelley's body, after he drowned while sailing with friends off the coast of Italy (from Edward John Trelawny's *Recollections of the Last Days of Shelley and Byron*):

> The limbs did not separate from the trunk as in the case of [another of the drowning victim's] body, so that the corpse was removed entire into the furnace. I had taken the precaution of having more and larger pieces of timber, in consequence of my experience of the day before ... After the fire was well kindled we repeated the ceremony of the previous day; and more wine was poured over Shelley's dead body than he had consumed during his life. This with the oil and salt made the yellow flames glisten and quiver ... The corpse fell open

and the heart was laid bare. The frontal bone of the skull, where it had been struck with the mattock, fell off; and ... the brain literally seethed, bubbled, and boiled as in a cauldron, for a very long time ... The fire was so fierce as to produce a white heat on the iron, and to reduce its contents to gray ashes. The only portions that were not consumed were some fragments of bones, the jaw, and the skull, but what surprised us all was that the heart remained entire. In snatching this relic from the fiery furnace, my hand was severely burnt; and had anyone seen me do the act I should have been put into quarantine.

96

NEAR DEATH. Write a fragment of fiction about a character who thinks she is dead, but is not dead. Don't dwell on the wounds or sudden illness that might have made this person mistake life for death. Imagine what someone might think under these circumstances. Would her life flash before her eyes? Or would she focus on—even obsess over—the fact that she had not fed her dogs before she left the apartment? 750 words.

THE POET WILFRED OWEN was shot and wounded during World War I. He passed out soon from loss of blood. He awoke to find himself slowly moving along under a clear blue sky—gentle motionless movement. He thought, "I am dead." It took him some time to gain the courage and energy to turn his head. He saw fields and forests drifting slowly past him. Eventually he realized he was on a barge being taken to a hospital. Seriously wounded patients usually hemorrhaged and died when ambulances drove them to hospitals over the rough, bombed-out roads of the front. Ninety percent of these soldiers died in ambulances; only 50 percent died on the barges. Owen did die a few months later, from other wounds, but perhaps his poetry, if he wrote any between this one injury and his last final one, was considerably elevated by the experience.

— **97**)———

9/11. Listen to three unnamed people on one of the upper floors of the World Trade Center on September 11, 2001, after the planes have crashed into the building but before they've fallen. Listen to these characters talk on the phone to their families (but don't let us hear the other side of the conversation). These people could be an executive, for example, a custodian, a receptionist, a mid-level manager, a stockbroker, or a paralegal. They are trapped. They have a little over an hour to live. They don't know how long they have to live, but they do know they're going to die. 500 words.

LIVING WITH THE CERTAINTY OF DEATH—not from natural causes but from some form of violence like this—is a rare situation. In the days after 9/11, what struck me was the phone messages on loved ones' answering machines from people in the buildings or on the planes. I could not think of another moment in time when so many people faced death and could speak about it to others at length. The handful of these messages I heard were remarkably calm, outward directed, perfectly aware of the fate that awaited them. We have an idea of how people are supposed to react when facing certain death. At least under these circumstances, in a building that had already been attacked by terrorists once eight years before, these voices were noble, loving, and efficient.

───────────── 98 ─────────────

FALLING OUT OF THE SKY. Write a very brief story about someone who has jumped from the burning top of one of the two towers of the World Trade Center on September 11, 2001.

It took the buildings each ten seconds to collapse, but I imagine it took less time for a person to fall to his death from these buildings. Watch Ric Burns's documentary about the building and destruction of these buildings to see a handful of video images of such falling men and women. Write about what the mind is experiencing while falling, although flashbacks are certainly possible (but try to avoid something like the Ambrose Bierce story "An Occurrence at Owl Creek Bridge," in which a man is hanged during the Civil War and the rope breaks and he dives into a river below him and swims to safety and runs away from the soldiers and finally reaches a long, beautiful tree-lined drive to an elegant home and sees his wife at the end of the drive only to have the rope yank him back to reality and death by noose and hanging).

Once you've written one of these stories, write another one and then a third one. Each story should be less than 250 words for a total of no more than 750 words.

───────────── 99 ─────────────

CARRYING A BODY. "I had been carrying the body of my friend for days." Use this sentence three times in a fragment of a story. Thanks to the poet Marc Gaba for this sentence. 500 words.

W ILL YOU TAKE THIS sentence literally? Or will you take it as a metaphor for some-thing else? I'd prefer you take it literally, but if you can come up with something that makes this sentence and thought reasonable and plausible, go ahead and do it. A woman could interpret this sentence as having something to do with pregnancy. Carrying a body of a friend for a few days? The last few days or weeks of the pregnancy might be the time when the mother begins to feel her child as a separate person, although I have no idea if that's true.

100

THE COMA. Write from the point of view of a person in a coma. This is a permanent condition. The patient will probably never come out of the coma but still haltingly comprehends the outer world. The voices of loved ones are familiar, even intimately familiar, but the comatose character cannot at-tach names to the voices. The patient has lost this capacity. 500 words.

T HIS IS AN EXERCISE about death-in-life. The person who is telling us this story is technically alive and is obviously narrating the tale for us—to us—but people in the room with him do not really know if the comatose person is alive or dead. This is also simply an exercise in sensory depriva-tion, like Plato's cave—shadows thrown against the wall of a character's consciousness. The people in this piece will be barely human—they'll be words, perhaps an odor, maybe a dim memory evoked.

101

A MASSACRE. Write about a massacre. Use no names. Make no men-tion of who the attackers are ethnically or who the attacked are. All of the people being attacked are killed, except for one, the narrator. Describe the lay of the land very carefully. 750 words.

TRY NOT TO GLORIFY this situation. It should not be fun to read. Be realistic and straightforward. Don't enjoy the mayhem, even if that's a temptation (I have to say, if you do enjoy describing death and violence—I don't approve). Take this massacre for what it is—a horrifying set of events in which a very large number of people are not only killed but die painfully and horribly.

102

XENOPHOBIA. Imagine an island (five miles by two miles) where the ancient inhabitants have not had contact with outsiders for centuries. Their ancestors built sharp projecting devices all around the island that cripple all incoming canoes (and which the contemporary inhabitants repair from time to time—perilous work). The islanders kill any survivors who happen to make it ashore when their canoes are wrecked. The island is in the middle of a very large lake, like one of the Great Lakes in North America. The islanders are completely self-sufficient. One day a bigger boat arrives, perhaps made of metal, so it is unscathed by the wooden spikes around the perimeter of the island. What happens next? 1,000 words.

I AM PROVIDING MUCH MORE PLOT than I usually do in these exercises. The problem here only loosely has to do with death, but a good deal of blood will be shed in whatever story you come up with. What you may prefer to entertain yourself with is the question of how to describe a community or just one person of this community who has so little exposure to the outside world. Would contact with others mean, all by itself, death?

---(103)---

KILLING THE PARENTS. A teenage child plots to kill her parents. Tell us the story from the point of view of the child just before the murder (for 250 words), making the act she is about to commit seem necessary and right. Then tell the story from the parents' point of view just after the act, stoutly defending their own behavior, appalled by their child's monstrosity, trying to come to terms with the love they still feel for this daughter, all the while slowly dying. Break up each section with titles, like Billie's Story and Mr. and Mrs. Wilson's Story. 500 words.

I AM SORRY FOR DREAMING up this exercise. I don't generally approve of this kind of subject matter. When Lyle and Erik Menendez killed their parents in 1989, I was only slightly interested, perhaps because a girlfriend of mine at the time had been at Princeton around the same time Lyle was. *Oedipus Rex* and *Hamlet*, to name just two works of literature, cover some of this same ground, and Sigmund Freud was impressed by both plays. In *Schnitzler's Century*, Peter Gay describes what drove Freud to name his famous complex after the earlier work: "He placed great weight on the fact that the protagonist of *Oedipus Rex* acts out his incestuous passions while Shakespeare's Hamlet represses them."

---(104)---

THE FUN IN FUNERAL. The narrator of this exercise slips into a funeral uninvited. Every character at this event you're describing will be a stranger to the narrator. So any description of these mourners will have to be speculative, based on clothing, body type, gestures, the handful of phrases these people speak that the narrator can reasonably over-hear (if he speaks directly to the mourners he risks being exposed as a voyeur). The exercise is about the social dynamic of a funeral, but it should also be about this narrator's ethics and emotional makeup. Why would someone do this? How could he get away with it? Is it a once-only lark or a common behavior? 500 words.

In Owen Wilson and Vince Vaughn's silly and occasionally funny film *Wedding Crashers*, Will Ferrell makes a cameo appearance at the end. He is the master who taught them both how to seek out strangers' weddings, do enough research to be able to attend without drawing too much attention to themselves, and therefore take advantage of the attractive women guests who want nothing more than to forget about marriage and fall into bed with attractive men. Will Ferrell has become (or degenerated into) a person who crashes funerals, at this point. It is a much easier pastime, presumably. He doesn't need to do research. Everyone is grieving and probably won't notice the stranger lurking around the edges, making small talk with the appealing widow.

DYING YOUNG. Write a fragment of a story about a character who is relatively young (under forty), who will die in a few years but has no inkling of this. You as author do know, but the reader should not know of the character's future untimely death. The death will not be an accident. It will be the result of this character's lifestyle and choices. 500 words.

In *Cutty, One Rock*, August Kleinzahler tells the story of his older brother, Harris, whose life played out like a romantic poet's—except that Harris was a financial analyst by day and a hustler by night. Harris, whose preferred beverage was Cutty Sark Scotch with a single ice cube, committed suicide at twenty-seven. "It's not as if he didn't understand that much of his behavior was driven by desperation and self-hate," Kleinzahler wrote. "He wasn't shallow or unreflective, quite the contrary. It was simply the way he was. He was born wild, born troubled. He wasn't designed for the long haul; not everyone is."

RELIGION

I am not a believer, but all religions fascinate (and sometimes horrify) me. The act of praying strikes me as being a fundamentally human act, even if prayer to one deity is a relatively recent phenomenon. If you are religious, don't be shy of exploring both your own rituals and the community of others you can't imagine. The same goes for you unbelievers (a phrase that was thrown at me in Egypt, and I didn't like it, but now I find it a bit more palatable and descriptive). Study people and groups of people you don't know, as well as your own tribe. Ask questions. Take notes. Observe the way strangers and friends cope with the terrors of the world.

— 106 —

PRIVATE PRAYER. Write about someone who quietly prays throughout a story fragment. Don't let these prayers be visible, audible, or obvious to any other character in the piece of fiction. The prayers can be religious and orthodox, but they can also be very secular. Devote a good deal of narrative thought to the process of these prayers. How do they fit in with the plot of the story you're writing? How can they fit? 750 words.

THE BIBLE (MATTHEW 6:5-6) gives this advice about public vs. private prayer:

> When you pray, be not like the pretenders, who prefer to pray in the synagogues and in the public square, in the sight of others. In truth I tell you, that is all the profit they will have. But you, when you pray, go into your inner chamber and, locking the door, pray there in hiding to your Father, and your Father who sees you in hiding will reward you.

───────────────── **107** ─────────────────

AMERICAN RAMADAN. Imagine an event or moment that causes everyone in the United States (or in an American city) to experience the same thing at the same time. Ramadan is the Muslim observance held during the ninth month of the Muslim calendar. Fasting is observed from sunrise to sunset. All who practice this faith know that everyone else is doing the same thing—fasting or breaking the fast—at the same time. Contemplate a fictional moment like the sunset when a whole city is turned toward prayer and then a light meal (see below). Is something like this possible in the multicultural, multireligious United States? Try to imagine it. 750 words.

WHEN I LIVED IN CAIRO, the first night of Ramadan surprised me. I lived in a top-floor apartment in a densely populated wealthy neighborhood. The great surprise of Ramadan was how quiet the city became in the half an hour or so before sunset, which marked the end of the day-long fast. Cairo is otherwise the noisiest city I've ever lived in—because nearly every driver honks his car horn constantly. Everyone had rushed to be home by sunset, to be with family, for this first light meal. I heard the cannon shot, from a hill on the other side of the city, and then I heard complete silence. A moment or two later, I heard the distinct sound of silverware hitting plates—people eating all around me. I could see, through the nearest apartment windows, dozens of people gathered around dining room tables. I'd been in Cairo for nine months, and I had never felt so alone and homesick as I did at that moment.

There is nothing quite like Ramadan in the United States. Thanksgiving happens at no set time of day. Christmas is also celebrated in varying fashions, the night before, the morning, and the big meal also roams from midday to evening. The events most similar to Ramadan, which bring the country together, are tragedies—the Kennedy and Martin Luther King, Jr. assassinations, 9/11. But we are not brought together in harmony. Even New Year's Eve is celebrated with the movement of the planet, and it is a secular, bacchanalian festival. Be serious about this. Don't imagine something like a large-scale season finale to *American Idol* or *The Sopranos*.

108

THE DEVIL'S HOLIDAY. Imagine a contemporary devil—someone who loves to lie and confuse—on holiday. He wears a T-shirt that says on the front, "The statement on the back is false" and the back of the T-shirt says, "The statement on the front is true." Your devil, for whatever reasons of his own, prefers not to be known by mortal humans for what he is, at least during a brief vacation among men. Ignore the images you've seen of this creature from Hollywood (much as I like Elizabeth Hurley's interpretation in *Bedazzled*). Don't go for the bells and whistles. Stay simple and modest. Remember that when seventeenth-century poet John Milton wrote *Paradise Lost* ("to justify the ways of God to men"), he became so enamored of the devil he may have sided with "the Devil's party without knowing it" (so said Blake). Milton's devil is rebellious, against authority, a rabble-rouser. He is not the personification of evil. 500 words.

AMBROSE BIERCE WROTE a whole book for this mythical figure, *The Devil's Dictionary*. Here are a few definitions:

> *Christian.* One who believes that the New Testament is a divinely inspired book admirably suited to the spiritual needs of his neighbor. One who follows the teachings of Christ in so far as they are not inconsistent with a life of sin.

> *Heaven.* A place where the wicked cease from troubling you with talk of their personal affairs, and the good listen with attention while you expound your own.

On January 1, 2006, Pope Benedict XVI spoke about the consequences of lies:

> ... Sacred Scripture, in its very first book, Genesis, points to the lie told at the very beginning of history by the animal with a forked tongue, whom the Evangelist John calls "the father of lies" (John 8:44). Lying is also one of the sins spoken of in the final chapter

of the last book of the Bible, Revelation, which bars liars from the heavenly Jerusalem: "outside are ... all who love falsehood" (22:15). Lying is linked to the tragedy of sin and its perverse consequences, which have had, and continue to have, devastating effects on the lives of individuals and nations. We need but think of the events of the past century, when aberrant ideological and political systems willfully twisted the truth and brought about the exploitation and murder of an appalling number of men and women, wiping out entire families and communities. After experiences like these, how can we fail to be seriously concerned about lies in our own time, lies which are the framework for menacing scenarios of death in many parts of the world.

Try to reconcile these two philosophies.

— **109** —

THE PRIEST. Write a letter from a priest or a minister or a rabbi or a mullah in a community of observant and religious people. This person has committed a crime and knows he will be punished soon. The letter can be addressed to the priest's parish or to some individual who has been wronged or to a supervisor. 500 words.

WALTER BENJAMIN, IN HIS TRAVEL ESSAY "NAPLES," captures the esteem with which priests used to be held, even when they were corrupt:

> Some years ago a priest was drawn on a cart through the streets of Naples for indecent offenses. He was followed by a crowd hurling maledictions. At a corner a wedding procession appeared. The priest

stands up and makes the sign of a blessing, and the cart's pursuers fall on their knees. So absolutely, in this city, does Catholicism strive to reassert itself in every situation. Should it disappear from the face of the earth, its last foothold would perhaps not be Rome, but Naples.

110

THE APOCALYPSE. Heinrich Heine said, "Holland is always fifty years behind the times, so if I hear the world is about to end, I'll go to Holland." Write a comedy about the end of the world. 666 words.

111

THE WATCHTOWER. Write a story about three people who belong to charismatic sect like the Jehovah's Witnesses or an Assembly of God (Pentecostal) church. They accept fervently and without irony this evangelical faith. Their religious faith should not be the central concern of this story, but it should underlie everything they speak about and believe in. 750 words.

YEARS AGO IN THE BROOKLYN HEIGHTS editorial offices of the *Watchtower*, at the Jehovah's Witnesses headquarters, two men were looking out at Wall Street in Manhattan across the East River, when a large thunderstorm threatened. They were quiet for a few minutes, and then one said to the other, "You think this is it?" They meant the Apocalypse, the end of the world. They were almost excited at the notion of its imminent arrival. This is one small example of the worldview of this community, which I believe I read in an essay by a disaffected former Jehovah's Witness.

——————————————— 112 ———————————————

AN AMERICAN IN MECCA. There is a huge sign on the multilane highway leading to Mecca that says, "Unbelievers Exit Here." There is another sign that says, "Believers Straight Ahead." Imagine an American Muslim (or more dangerously an American masquerading as a Muslim) who travels into Mecca during the season of the Haj, when millions of Muslims from around the world converge on Mecca. Anyone who somehow gets into Mecca who is not a Muslim is liable to be punished by death, if found out. 500 words.

——————————————— 113 ———————————————

UNBELIEVERS EXIT HERE. Write an essay about a moment of sudden spiritual doubt. The fact that this is an essay does not mean it has to be a truthful piece of writing. It could be from your own experience, or it could be told by a fictional character. But stay within the comfortable confines of the genre of the essay. 750 words.

IN THE PREVIOUS EXERCISE An American in Mecca (112), I described the sign on the highway toward Mecca in Saudi Arabia that says, "Unbelievers Exit Here." Has there been a similar specific point in your own life where you've faced something like this road sign? This does not have to be about religious belief. A memoir is a study of the moments in a life you can remember or for which you have documentary evidence (a journal, a marriage, a degree, a house, a set of travels, a business ledger). What and why do we remember? Islam seems a more fierce religion these days than Christianity, but its simple divide between belief and unbelief (which Christians used to kill over) is a fine point, when you think about it in secular terms.

At what point did you stop (or start) believing in Santa Claus, God, romantic love, fad diets, the basic goodness of human beings? Choose what beliefs to write about idiosyncratically well, and you'll have the beginnings of a lovely personal essay. I have been writing lately about my own ideas on religion, especially in relation to Islam, because I lived in Egypt for two years in the 1980s and I had to answer the simple question from Muslim friends and strangers, "What are you?" I found that saying "atheist" provoked too many other questions, and I also began to realize that I was, like it or not, a Christian, at least in the sense that my language and the basis of my worldview were Christian (I shout out, "Jesus Christ!" when I hit my thumb with a hammer). I've also been trying to define what philosophy means to me, because my father is a philosopher. It's been interesting to trace my notions of and anxieties about this first field of study over the years I've been aware that there was a field of study called *philosophy* that was more than just my father's day job.

Willing suspension of disbelief is supposed to be a crucial readerly activity in fiction. The old argument was that if you thought you were reading a piece of fiction, the fiction could not be properly experienced or was not effective as fiction. Suspension of disbelief is more or less a double negative of belief, which is the foundation of the essay and personal nonfiction (as opposed to the kind of nonfiction Tracy Kidder writes, for example, in which the author of the piece is erased from the telling, in most cases—in which the activities of the book are more important than the narration). In a personal essay, belief is the key. Who believes you, as author? Why do they believe you? What and when did you start or stop believing certain tenets and golden rules? Life is a series of moments of sudden or gradual belief or disbelief. This exercise attempts to guide writers toward describing these moments and perhaps piecing together a narrative pattern of your life.

114

RITUAL & DISORDER. Examine two small sets of characters. One group is very ritualistic and adores familiar patterns and repetitions. The other group revels (or simply exists) in a state of chaos or disorder. What happens when these two groups encounter each other for a prolonged period of time in a relatively confined space? 750 words.

IN A 1954 ISSUE OF *TIME* magazine, a few of one writer's rituals are described:

> For Ernest Hemingway, when he is writing, every day begins in that private world. As early as 5:30 in the morning, before any but some gabby bantams and a few insomniac cats are awake, he goes to work in the big main bedroom of his villa. He writes standing up at the mantelpiece, using pencil for narrative and description, a typewriter for dialogue "in order to keep up."

"Ritual recognizes the potency of disorder," the anthropologist Mary Douglas dryly notes. Most writers have a rage for order, as Hemingway did. But ritual and habit are also two of the great subjects of narrative.

Here is what follows the line above, from the Mary Douglas book *Purity and Danger:*

> In the disorder of the mind, in dreams, faints, and frenzies, ritual expects to find powers and truths which cannot be reached by conscious effort. Energy to command and special powers of healing come to those who can abandon rational control for a time. Sometimes an Andaman Islander leaves his band and wanders in the forest like a madman. When he returns to his senses and to human society he has gained occult power of healing.

SCIENCE

When I started my first novel (which I never finished) about sabotage at the Indian Point nuclear power plant a few dozen miles north of New York City, I was surprised by how much fun I had with the research. In fact, the subject of the novel did not intrigue me nearly as much as the research I had to do—on the effects of nuclear radiation, the mass movement of human beings during environmental catastrophes, and even the physics of nuclear power itself. If you are a writer, you are probably intimidated by the hard sciences. Don't be. Explore the subject, especially if you are writing a problem that science can solve.

——————————— 115)———————————

RETINAL ENNUI. Write a part of a story in which a stationary object sits or stands at the center of the story's vision. Make this stationary object intriguing, but don't pay too much attention to it. Eventually something about this object becomes important to the story. It comes to have meaning to the characters that have been walking past it and taking it for granted for some time. 500 words.

MARKUS MEISTER IN *HARVARD MAGAZINE* describes something called *retinal ennui*. Ennui is boredom—or dramatically elevated boredom. "The eye's retina—in animals as diverse as rabbits and salamanders—focuses on 'difference' as we scan the landscape. The retina de-emphasizes recurring features, like the relatively static and nonthreatening trees, while keying in on the mobile and potentially lethal tiger." You stare at one image long enough and your vision begins to blur. Describing an object that also should not stand out at first will be challenging. You might break the object down into parts, which you can evoke without paying too much attention to the larger whole.

──────────────(**116**)──────────────

CAMOUFLAGE. Write a short scene about a person who uses some-thing like the markings on the top of a flounder that look like pebbles and sand. The simplest form of camouflage in nature is to blend in with the background. Your character needs a kind of disguise that matches the background—not a vertically striped outfit to blend in with striped wall-paper, but some sort of outfit that makes her fade into the crowd. Why would this character need a disguise? Is she a private eye on the trail of a client's husband? Is she a spy? Is she an undercover cop? The intent of this exercise is to show us the actions of a person who not only does not want to stand out but works at blending into the crowd. Figuring out how to make a fictional character blend in will be your primary task in this exercise. 500 words.

THE WORD *CAMOUFLAGE* came from a French factory during World War I. The factory painted over its roof to look from the air as if a road were passing through the area uninterrupted. Animals have evolved special adaptations that help them find food and keep them from becoming food. The larva of a swallowtail butterfly has huge staring eyes that intimidate predators. Younger larvae of the same species have markings that imitate bird droppings. Vladimir Nabokov, in *The Gift*, displays a sample of human camouflage: "Striped and spotted with words, dressed in verbal camouflage, the important idea he wished to convey would slip through."

PERFECT WEATHER. Donald Barthelme used to say, "Never open a story with a description of the weather." In this exercise, I want you to open a story with a description of the weather. In the movie *L.A. Story*, there is an electronic weather report on a highway billboard that says, "Sunny and warmer, next report in four days." Unless the weather is very bad, it rarely plays an interesting role in the fiction we read and write. Glorious weather is invisible unless you're writing about two young lovers out for a stroll through fields of lavender. Make perfect weather visible and important for this story. 500 words.

DO SOME RESEARCH into the science of weather. Find some enjoyable vocabulary to throw into the pot with the other ordinary language of your piece. For example, here's something from my brother's 1967 book *Weather* by

Armand Spitz: "The most common, most observed, most easily recognized cloud is the *cumulus humilis*, the cumulus of fair weather. This cloud may appear almost isolated in an absolutely clear sky, or it may be accompanied by others like itself. Formulations are most frequently seen from about noon, when warm updrafts have been set into motion by insolation." This lovely last word (*insolation*) means exposure of something to sunlight.

118

UFO. Write a sequence of brief, stunned descriptions of one person's close encounter of the second kind—an observation of a UFO. The event isn't recollected in tranquility—it has just happened to this character. 500 words.

WIKIPEDIA OFFERS SOME of the effects witnesses have described of this kind of encounter:

> Heat or radiation
> Damage to the terrain
> Human paralysis
> Frightened animals
> Interference with engines or TV or radio reception

Whether you believe in this stuff or not, be faithful to this observer's experience of panic and disorientation.

Charles Euchner, in an essay for *Newsweek* about UFO sightings, gave a possible explanation for occasional mass sightings:

> For all but the last ten thousand years of human history, man survived by hunting and gathering plants. To interpret a mysterious

world, man projected his own fears and understandings onto his environment. In the "enchanted" view of the world, every part of nature—rocks, trees, hills, water—was alive and filled with spirit. Even in the age of science, the human brain still projects ideas and images on the world ...

Euchner rationalizes the experience of UFO sightings by looking into the minds of the witnesses, rather than out into the sky and space: "When people see something they cannot explain—which might happen more frequently in a noisy environment—they use images stored in the brain to complete the picture and make sense of it." He also notes that one common thread among these witnesses is that they frequently suffer from sleep deprivation. Euchner clearly does not believe that UFOs exist. Fiction has fun with things that are not supposed to exist.

119

THAT'S LIFE. Write a very short story from the point of view of an alien, or an at-least-up-to-now unknown life form that is observing human behavior. This life form is not humanoid. It is not in any way like humans, actually. It could be algae-like, or a cloud of radiation, or a rock that isn't a rock. Don't dwell on the particulars of this life form. The alien may not be able to describe itself, and why would it want to? Spend your energies trying to imagine how human behavior looks to this radically different form of intelligence. The alien, by the way, has no intention (or capability) of harming or even interacting with humans. 750 words.

In "Are Aliens Among Us?" (from *Scientific American*), Paul Davies says:

> If life, so famously problematic to define, is said to be a system having a property—such as the ability to store and process certain kinds of information—that marks a well-defined transition from the nonliving to the living realm, it would be meaningful to talk about one or more origin-of-life events. If, however, life is weakly defined as something like organized complexity, the roots of life may meld seamlessly into the realm of general complex chemistry. It would then be a formidable task to demonstrate independent origins for different forms of life unless the two types of organisms were so widely separated that they could not have come into contact (for instance, if they were located on planets in different star systems).

— 120)—

SMELL IS EMOTIONAL. Write a short short story about two people who were once in love, years before. They meet by accident after years of no contact, and when we see them they are enjoying a brief meal together. Some odor enters the restaurant or cafe they're seated in, and this smell triggers intense memories for one of the characters (but not the other). Examine from many angles the effects of this experience of being taken back in time by a smell. You'll have to do some practical research yourself—gathering together items that have distinctive aromas that could be triggers. Describe them. Compare the smells to other smells or to sounds or colors. 500 words.

SIGHT IS EVIDENCE, smell is emotion. What we see, we believe. What about what we smell? Smell often provokes memories. Smell evokes danger, lust, hunger, yearning. Humans walk into a room and after a time can't smell what they smelled at first. Dogs don't have scent fatigue.

In his *New Yorker* review of *Perfumes: The Guide* by Luca Turin and Tania Sanchez, John Lanchester talks about the science of smell (whose mysteries may derive from the fact that we're not dogs):

> The tongue can detect only five tastes, salty, sweet, bitter, sour, and a taste whose receptors have only begun to be identified: umami—the savory, brothy sensation that is amply present in Parmesan, seaweed, and ripe tomatoes. The rest is smell ... So taste is mainly smell, and smell is a profound mystery. Why is it that one molecule smells of spearmint, while its mirror image smells of caraway? No one knows. When scientists create new molecules in the laboratory, they may know every detail of a molecule's structure yet have no clue about what it will smell like.

Here's one of Luca Turin's reviews of a perfume:

> I once sat in the London Tube across from a young woman in a T-shirt printed with headline-sized words "ALL THIS" across her large breasts, and in small type underneath "and brains too." That vulgar-but-wily combination seems to me to sum up Trésor. Up close, when you can read the small print, Trésor is a superbly clever accord between powdery rose and vetiver, reminiscent of the structure of Habanita. From a distance, it's the trashiest, most good-humored pink mohair sweater and bleached hair thing

imaginable. When you manage to appeal to both the reptilian brain and the neocortex of menfolk, what happens is what befell Trésor: a huge success.

——————————— 121)———————————

THE TARANTULA HAWK. Here's another of Dan Wiencek's "Thirteen Writing Prompts" from *McSweeney's*: "A wasp called the tarantula hawk reproduces by paralyzing tarantulas and laying its eggs into their bodies. When the larvae hatch, they devour the still living spider from the inside out. Isn't that fucked up? Write a short story about how fucked up that is." 500 words.

ASIDE FROM THE LAST SENTENCE Dan Wiencek throws in, the information here is strange, chilling, scientifically accurate, and it is very hard to imagine a fiction writer being able to work with this information. I did work with this sort of information when I wrote *Still Life With Insects*, but that seems almost unfair. My narrator was a beetle collector. He'd tell stories a little like this one in passing, about other insects, but he was always a little protective of the subspecies he'd chosen to study, the beetle, which is the largest of the insect world. What can you do with a tarantula hawk? Could you use it as a metaphor for ugly human behavior? Could this detail show up in your story undigested?

POLITICS

In his essay "On Political Judgment," Isaiah Berlin writes that wise leaders don't think abstractly. They use powers of close observation to integrate the vast shifting amalgam of data that constitute their own particular situation—their own and no other.

Don't be afraid to express political opinions in your fiction—your own opinions or other people's opinions. Timid fiction—apolitical fiction—is a waste of our time, in the end. Engage with the world. Give your characters strong convictions, even if they are wrong-headed. As an aside, I cannot believe there is anyone out there who does not vote (or even vote regularly). Register to vote, and vote early and often. These are perilous times, and we must elect responsible, reasonable, and intelligent politicians (even if that sometimes seems like a contradiction in terms).

WHAT DEMOCRACY MEANS TO ME. Write a fragment of a political statement made by someone who ordinarily does not make political statements. This person has his own political ideas and ideals, but he rarely (or perhaps never) expresses them aloud. But for this little moment, this speech, give this person a reason to vent. All we'll hear, in this exercise, is the person's voice and words, not the context of the speech (it could be at a party, at Thanksgiving dinner among strangers, in a classroom, at a bus stop—it doesn't matter where, but I want you to keep that information to yourself). How will you make it clear from this speech that this person doesn't ordinarily speechify about politics? That's your main job here. The speaker could just say so: "I don't like to talk politics. I'm pretty stupid on the topic. I don't read newspapers or magazines. I don't have any political blogs among my Favorites." Or you could just ignore the preamble and get to the heart of the matter. 250 words.

JOHNNY CARSON ONCE GAVE this apparently serious talk on *The Tonight Show*, which he called "What Democracy Means to Me":

> Democracy is buying a big house you can't afford with money you don't have to impress people you wish were dead. And, unlike communism, democracy does not mean having just one ineffective political party; it means having two ineffective political parties ... Democracy is welcoming people from other lands, and giving them something to hold onto—usually a mop or a leaf blower. It means that with proper timing and scrupulous bookkeeping, anyone can die owing the government a huge amount of money ... Democracy means free television, not good television, but free ... And finally, democracy is the eagle on the back of a dollar bill, with thirteen arrows in one claw, thirteen leaves on a branch, thirteen tail feathers, and thirteen stars over its head—this signifies that when the white man came to this country, it was bad luck for the Indians, bad luck for the trees, bad luck for the wildlife, and lights out for the American eagle. I thank you.

Really what Johnny Carson is referring to here is American democracy. He wrote this in the 1970s. Carson was not a political comic or host, as his rival Dick Cavett sometimes seemed to be. But he could occasionally come out with this sort of blast, which has a good deal of political cynicism behind it.

--- **123** ---

ONE SHIT AT A TIME. Write a fragment of a story about an American President (or his Russian or Chinese counterpart) forced to meet with the leader of the opposition party, without anyone else in the room (there is no opposition party in China, but imagine one anyway). You don't have to put the President on the toilet (Lyndon Johnson liked to talk with opponents from his bathroom, with the door slightly ajar—he kept them off-balance this way). The conversation doesn't have to be about politics, strictly, but you can imagine that everything said in this moment would be political. 500 words.

WINSTON CHURCHILL WAS SITTING on the toilet when his manservant told him the leader of the opposition party was in the sitting room. Churchill said, "I can take only one shit at a time." This sort of brutality is refreshing to imagine and play with. The supreme power that Churchill, Johnson, Abraham Lincoln, or Augustus Caesar had gave them the freedom to speak without censorship, even when they were joking. Lyndon Johnson's famous quip about some political rival is further evidence of this: "He can't pour piss out of a boot with the instructions printed on the heel." And: "I wouldn't piss down his throat if his heart was on fire." Writers yearn for this kind of completely unrepressed voice.

--- **124** ---

THE NEGATIVE MASTER NARRATIVE. Try out the method of creating a negative story about an opponent on a small scale. Imagine Karl Rove or James Carville (or this kind of political operative) in high school or in the second year of college. Imagine someone like Rove or Carville, who wants to date a woman, but he has to spread negative master narratives about his rival for the hand of this woman. 500 words.

IN THE *HUFFINGTON POST*, Kirsten Powers talks about the method some politicians use to undermine their opponents:

> Republicans test out different negative narrative threads about Democratic candidates in an attempt to caricature some minor trait—real or imagined—that they have determined American voters will reject. Reporters latch onto the caricature because they like themes. Before you know what happened, the average American voter is claiming John Kerry seems "French" (read: not like me) or that Al Gore lies and exaggerates and claims he invented the Internet (which he never said).

Evan Thomas, in *Newsweek*, writes about "The 'Myth' of Media Objectivity":

> The mainstream media (the "MSM" the bloggers love to rail against) are prejudiced, but not ideologically. The press's *real* bias is for conflict. Editors, even ones who marched in antiwar demonstrations during the Vietnam era, have a weakness for war, the ultimate conflict. Inveterate gossips and snoops, journalists also share a yen for scandal, preferably sexual. But mostly they are looking for narratives that reveal something of character. It is the human drama that most compels our attention.

So the press and political operatives work hand-in-hand creating narratives, though often unwittingly.

—————————————— **125** ——————————————

DOUBT. Write a short scene involving at least three people in which one of the characters is trying to convince the others of some simple falsehood by means of doubt. This does not have to be a political discussion. Say the other people are absolutely sure of the directions to a party and the protagonist (or, technically, the antagonist) doesn't want to go to this party. She uses doubt to throw everyone else off their certainty, to confuse their sense of the directions to this neighborhood and house, the way Brown & Williamson did for years to sow doubt about the real and obvious dangers of cigarette smoking. 750 words.

A BROWN & WILLIAMSON TOBACCO CORPORATION memo explained this philosophy with great bluntness, decades ago: "Doubt is our product, since it is the best means of competing with the 'body of fact' that exists in the mind of the general public."

—————————————— **126** ——————————————

REPUBLICANS. Write a short conversation with pauses for activity and thought between two smart young Republicans. They are talking politics. A third character enters the scene and attacks their arguments unfairly, without any self-control. Dip into the epithets that Garrison Keillor hurls at this American political party (below) to provoke a response from your fictional characters. Think up more angry insults like these, and let them sit at the heart of a conversation these characters have. 500 words.

GARRISON KEILLOR DESCRIBED REPUBLICANS a little jokingly (but with a hard edge), in *Salon* in 2006:

> I recall having once referred to Republicans as "hairy-backed swamp developers, fundamentalist bullies, freelance racists, hobby cops, sweatshop tycoons, line jumpers, marsupial moms and aluminum-siding salesmen, misanthropic frat boys, ninja dittoheads, shrieking midgets, tax cheats, cheese merchants, cat stranglers, pill pushers, nihilists in golf pants, backed-up Baptists, the grand pooh-bahs of Percodan, mouth breathers, testosterone junkies, and brownshirts in pinstripes." I look at those words now, and "cat stranglers" seems excessive to me. The number of cat stranglers in the ranks of the Republican Party is surely low, and that reference was hurtful to Republicans and to cat owners. I feel sheepish about it.

I'm attacking Republicans a good deal in this section. I have a right to my own opinions. But what I want to provoke here is not agreement. I want to provoke potent political attitudes in your fiction, at least some of the time.

127

WAR STORIES. Retell in your own details this story from Ken Burns's documentary on World War II. A man in a foxhole listens to a fellow soldier who's been shot, dying slowly during a terrifying night in which all the American soldiers think they are facing a large Japanese onslaught. He wishes only for this man to die. The next morning, his platoon discovers that there were no Japanese soldiers anywhere nearby, that the gunshot that killed this soldier was fired, inadvertently, by one of the Americans, and that the man who died was the best friend of the soldier telling this story. This is a prototypical war story—the mad, confusing, heartbreaking unreality of the experience, which few survivors can tell to family and friends at home. Instead of World War II, put these soldiers in Iraq, several years after President Bush stood on the USS Abraham Lincoln below the *Mission Accomplished* banner on May 1, 2003. 750 words.

WHY HAVE I PLACED THIS EXERCISE in the Politics exercises? War is politics by other means, Carl von Clausewitz said, and Mao said that war is politics with bloodshed. On NPR in 2007, Gary Trudeau said a few days after he published the newspaper comic strip of *Doonesbury* in which his long-running character B.D. had his leg blown off in Iraq, he got a call from the Pentagon. They said, "It looks like you're going to be in this story for the long term. Let us know if there's anything we can do to help." Trudeau flew down to Washington the next day. This is an example of the way politics, the military, and the media intermingle in weird and delightful ways.

George Feifer, in his book *The Battle of Okinawa*, describes the essence of the experience of war:

> War's horror exists partly because outsiders can't know it. "If people really knew, the war would be stopped tomorrow," said Prime Minister David Lloyd George in 1916, when trench warfare [was at its most brutal and murderous] ... Not even servicemen know, since a minute proportion of them actually fight—and those who do are unlikely to describe their ordeal, partly because few are writers, partly because all rightly believe no one who hasn't experienced combat

can imagine it. As a historian of battle recently put it, combat is "too little related to anything recognizably human or natural."

—————————— 128) ——————————

GOOD & EVIL. Imagine two characters that fit Simone Weil's descriptions of real evil and real good (below). Put them in a low-level political situation—a high school presidential election; a city council campaign in a small city; a battle between two co-workers over a promotion to management. In other words, put these characters in a set of circumstances that is not life-or-death. 750 words.

SIMONE WEIL SAID, "Imaginary evil is romantic and varied; real evil is gloomy, monotonous, barren, boring. Imaginary good is boring; real good is always new, marvelous, intoxicating." Writers have a tendency to idealize evil and dismiss goodness. Don't do that. Most of us, I hope, have very little real contact with truly evil people. We see little bits and pieces of it. We see much more goodness than we realize, too.

I personally tend to apply these terms to politics much more than to real life. I've said in conversation more than once that George W. Bush and Dick Cheney are pure evil. I'm sure they have qualities their wives and children and friends adore, but I am equally sure history will judge this administration the worst in American history. I also felt that my old political science professor and later Senator from Minnesota, Paul Wellstone, was the personification of good. My point is that politics—both on the national level and on the level of a group of twenty workers trying to decide on a leader—tends to exaggerate this dichotomy. See what happens to someone who has poor social skills when he tries to run for a position of small power. I had bosses in my nine-to-five jobs in the 1980s who were routinely petty, secretive, insecure, and difficult to work for. All of the people who worked for these bosses thought of them, at one time or another, as at least a little bit evil. They weren't. Try to distinguish between evil and incompetent (or only intermittently competent).

JOKES

Bob Newhart, in *I Shouldn't Even Be Doing This*, tries to define his art:

> Comedy is a way to bring logic to an illogical situation, of which there are many in everyday life ... A long time ago, I read a news item that illustrated this point nicely. An engineer at a Palm Springs TV station had a private porno tape that he was playing for his buddies in the late shift. Somehow, he accidentally transmitted the tape over the air. The strange thing was that the station didn't receive a single telephone call while the tape was playing, but the minute it was over, the phone lines lit up with outraged callers.

Woody Allen ends his movie *Annie Hall* with this joke:

> This guy goes to a psychiatrist and says, "Doc, my brother's crazy. He thinks he's a chicken." And the doctor says, "Why don't you turn him in?" And the guy says, "I would but I need the eggs."

The joke sums up how Allen's stand-in Alvy Singer feels about relationships: "They're totally irrational and crazy and absurd, but I

guess we keep going through it because most of us need the eggs."
In a review of *The Lazarus Project* by Aleksandar Hemon, Cathleen
Schine makes this lovely observation of how the structure of jokes
and humor can penetrate fiction at the level of its bones:

> Some writers turn despair into humor as a way of making
> the world bearable, of discovering some glimmer of beauty
> or pleasure or, most important, humanity. In contrast, the
> gifted Bosnian writer Aleksandar Hemon has taken the formal
> structure of humor, the grammar of comedy, the rhythms and
> beats of a joke, and used them to reveal despair.

129

META-HUMOR. Use meta-humor, which I've briefly tried to describe
below, in a short fragment of fiction for a serious, even grave, longer piece
you're working on. A few of the qualities of postmodern comedy are disregard for continuity, surreal connections, and speaking directly to the
audience in pretend sincerity. This approach to humor might be useful
for relief from a stressful situation. You might consider the sort of absurd
comedy something you yourself, as a writer, need, for any number of reasons. If the jokiness stands out too much, a gentle revision, later, might
turn this comic scene into just the right thing for the story. 250 words.

IN *SALON*, STEPHANIE ZACHAREK described her favorite Steve Martin routine, which was

> ... his lovelorn magician, the Great Flydini (an act Martin brought,
> memorably, to Johnny Carson's *The Tonight Show* in the last week

of its run). Flydini draws an array of objects—a string of brightly colored scarves, a few eggs, a glass of wine—from the fly of his pants. When he draws on a cigarette, smoke emerges, in gentle puffs, from his trousers; when a curvy cutie struts by, a lush bouquet pops out. But the woman rejects him, and so for the finale, a Pavarotti puppet emerges from between the zipper teeth, singing an aria of lost love and betrayal, an echo of the pained expression Martin wears on his face.

Steve Martin says, "What if there were no punch lines? What if I created tension and never released it? What if I headed for a climax, but all I delivered was an anticlimax?" This may be the heart of Steve Martin's original, philosophical, and postmodern humor. Another version of this sort of humor—or perhaps its mirror opposite—is Steven Wright's deadpan aphoristic humor—tiny little jokes that explode in your consciousness the moment they arrive or, occasionally, a few minutes later. Here are three examples:

> I think it's wrong that only one company makes the game *Monopoly*.

> I'm writing an unauthorized autobiography.

> A friend of mine has a trophy wife, but apparently it wasn't first place.

Wright delivers these nuggets of gags in a monotone, and he often does not pause for laughs. The jokes are very simple, and they also take an instant to comprehend, by which time he's moved on to the next joke-sentence. In his routines, Wright makes only a tiny pretense of telling a story. His models seem to be Bob Hope and Henny Youngman—a stream of brief unrelated anecdotes—"Take my wife, please" material. But Steven Wright updated their style slightly by the use of this monotonous delivery, and by the simple conceit of very obviously not trying to connect the tiny stories together. Comics in the 1970s, like Richard Pryor, began to tell long stories that had relatively few gags or punch lines. The situation itself was funny; the person telling the story honestly stood in front of you revealing himself. Pryor told horrifying tales of his own drug addiction, including lighting himself on fire and running down the street outside his home.

Wikipedia has a whole small section on meta-jokes. Here's one from that site: A man knocks on a farmer's door at night, and says, "I'm terribly sorry to bother you, but my car broke down. Can I stay the night?" The farmer says, "Sure, but you'll have to share a bed with my son." The man says, "Never mind, I must be in the wrong joke."

— **130** —

GUY WALKS INTO A BAR. Invent a half-dozen "guy walks into a bar ..." jokes, or type that phrase as a Google search and you'll find dozens of examples. Keep them short and to the point. Spread them throughout a story that has nothing to do with the jokes. Make the jokes completely unrelated to the story you're telling. Eventually, I suspect, you will find connections between these jokes and the nonjoking story. 750 words.

WHAT IS IT ABOUT JOKES that begin like this? Horse walks into a bar. Bartender says, "Why the long face?" A bar is a place where strangers meet, under the kind, wise guidance of a bartender. The key to jokes about bars is that the bartender and the customer are strangers to each other.

Why should this matter for a joke? Humor happens between intimates all the time, but humor between siblings or a married couple can be difficult for anyone else to access or understand. Many American bars are dimly lit, slightly lowlife places to be seen. Irish pubs have bright lighting, people talking in normal voices, kids running around underfoot. When I lived in Ireland in 1976, I did my schoolwork in a nearby pub because it was so much warmer than the home I was staying in, and because the community was welcoming. A ham sandwich walks into a bar and orders a drink. "I'm sorry," the bartender says. "We don't serve food here."

131

A PRACTICAL JOKE. A practical joke involves action rather than words, a joke played on someone, which turns the target of the joke into an actor or a character in a kind of theater. Have one of your fictional characters play a practical joke on another character. The second character is obviously unaware of being pranked. 500 words.

THE THEATRICALITY OF THIS PIECE is important to keep in mind as you work out its ramifications. It is easy to imagine a practical joke gone horribly wrong. It might be just as interesting to work out the planning that has to go into a successful practical joke. There would be a lot of variables to take into account—how to make the setup look plausible, who to recruit as actors, or where to perform the practical joke.

132

CONTROLLED INCONGRUITY. A doctor's receptionist tells him there's an invisible man in the waiting room. "Tell him I can't see him," the doctor says. It's an old joke. Make this the opening line of your story. The rest of your story should be serious and straightforward, not funny. It should not be some larger version of this joke. 500 words.

STEVEN JOHNSON, IN *DISCOVER MAGAZINE*, writes about an actual scientific experiment to find the funniest joke in the world. Here's the joke that won (and Johnson's explication of the joke):

> A couple of New Jersey hunters are out in the woods when one of them falls to the ground. He doesn't seem to be breathing; his eyes are rolled back in his head. The other guy whips out his cell phone and calls the emergency service. He gasps to the operator: "My friend is dead! What can I do?" The operator says: "Take it easy. I can help. First, let's make sure he's dead." There is silence, then a shot is heard. The guy's voice comes back on the line. He says, "OK, now what?"
>
> This joke illustrates the notion of controlled incongruity: You're expecting *x*, and you get *y*. In the hunting joke, there are two plausible ways to interpret the 911 operator's instructions—either the hunter should check his friend's pulse, or he should shoot him. The context sets you up to expect that he'll check his friend's pulse, so the—admittedly dark—humor arrives when he takes the more unlikely path.

—————————————— **133** ——————————————

THE IMPRESSIONIST. Write a short comic scene that involves more than four people. At the heart of the scene is one character doing a perfect imitation of another character in the room (or wherever you set this story-let). How on earth do you show an imitation like this in prose? Well, you could simply say the character is doing a perfect impression of the other character and leave it at that. Or you could work at the imitation. In any case, the act of mimicry should be at the center of some controversy in your piece of fiction. 750 words.

DAMON WAYANS DESCRIBED Richard Pryor's technical skill, after Pryor died: "There are many different kinds of comedians ... the observational humorist, the impressionist, the character creator, the physical comedian, the self-deprecator, and the dirty-joke teller. What made Richard Pryor so brilliant is he was able to incorporate all these styles at once."

An actor is always impersonating someone or something. Fiction writers often start out by doing imitations of other writers, but they develop their own voice and style over time. Can a fictional character sound like John Wayne or George W. Bush? Fiction doesn't usually traffic in this sort of voice recognition. But it would be interesting to try out a voice impression of some well-known character. Do this so it doesn't matter that we are being told a story in a Katharine Hepburn-imitation voice, for instance. All that matters is that you think you're mimicking the twang of her aristocratic Connecticut upbringing.

134

HE'S HAD ENOUGH. Write a piece of narrative that is both a very short story and an extended joke, using circular logic as your model. 500 words.

THE BOOK REVIEWER and political commentator James Wolcott retold this old joke in his political blog on July 15, 2006: "Shecky Greene tells about how Frank Sinatra saved his life. Seems that Shecky was being worked over in an alley by five goons when Frank looked over and said, 'OK—he's had enough.'" This is a kind of joke that depends on circular logic. We are watching a sort of tiny play. Shecky Greene is being beaten up. This by itself is disconcerting, but because we have so little else to go on we take it at face value. We know that Sinatra is responsible for "saving his life." At the end of the second sentence we learn that Sinatra was also responsible for the beating in the first place. At lightning speed, we get from point A to B and back to A again. Many jokes work this way, though few as efficiently as Shecky Greene's—or as Wolcott's witty condensation of the Greene joke, which is all punch line.

135

CARTOON TEXTS. Take a bunch of taglines from cartoons, say, from the *New Yorker*, such as: "It has great refracted light." "Beverly, brief me on my 11:15 duel." "Are you even listening to me?" "And then he turned the tranquilizer gun on himself." "Look, making you happy is out of the question, but I can give you a compelling narrative for your misery." "That was one strange and confusing competition." Put them together. You could also buy an old book of comics—*Peanuts*, *Calvin and Hobbes*, *Pogo*—and do the same thing, though you'd want to work against the grain of the stories of these more narrative comics. Type up ten or fifteen taglines and study them for a long while until they no longer seem connected to the comic strips they originally came from. Rearrange their order a few times until you can see a possible story between the taglines. Write some kind of narrative to link together these fragments of talk or description. 500 words.

TAKE A LOOK AT The Comics Curmudgeon (a witty and sarcastic "reading" of the days' newspaper cartoons—or selections thereof) at http://joshreads. com/. This is a wonderful site. Read it for your own amusement and edification, but also for all the comics you can use for the purpose of this exercise.

136

COMIC BALLOONS. Copy some pages of a narrative comic—*Archie*, *Spider-Man*, or your favorite manga or graphic novel. Blank out the text balloons with pieces of paper. Then make another copy of the comics so you have clean blank speech or thought balloons to work with. Now fill in these blank spaces with words that somehow fit the action being described on the pages of these comics. Eventually, type up the words from these comic strip balloons and integrate them into some kind of narrative of their own that has little or nothing to do with the story of the comic book. 500 words.

IN DAVID LEHMAN'S INTRODUCTION to Kenneth Koch's book *The Art of the Possible*, Lehman describes how Koch would have his students buy comic books, paper over the balloons, and add their own dialogue—"a great lesson in poetry as interpretation and mistranslation." Koch's lighthearted approach to poetry for children should be a lesson. *Interpretation* and *mistranslation* are heavy-duty words, but when they're applied to a process of rewriting comics they are both less serious and creatively playful.

The back of the *New Yorker* has a relatively new section in which there are three cartoons, one of which has no caption, one of which has three possible captions, and the final one of which has a winning caption (the captions are mailed in by readers of the magazine). The notion of this part of the magazine, as in Koch's experiment, is that there is no single story these images evoke, especially when there is only one image. This exercise is the opposite of Cartoon Texts (135).

137

STRAIGHT MAN. In the history of vaudeville, the straight man constantly protects his comic sidekick from the comic's messes. The comic creates chaos or danger for herself, perhaps because of the humor she uses, perhaps simply because of the way she moves through the world. Write a fragment of fiction from the point of view of a straight man (or woman). Your straight man may adore this funny companion or he may be dead tired of the jokes. Imagine what it would be like to have to tolerate (and be figuratively joined at the hip to) a comedian who can't ever be serious. 750 words.

IN VAUDEVILLE, THE STRAIGHT MAN was "relatively rational, compared to the comedian," according to *Vaudeville, Old and New: An Encyclopedia of Variety Performers in America*. Straight men were "the stand-ins for the audience." They anchored the "routine in plausibility, which the comedian constantly confounds ... The straight man functions as an interviewer, as much in control of the questions as the ... pace of the act."

HISTORY

In the end, history *is* writing. What we can experience of history, especially very distant history, is accessible only through words other people have written, in letters, journals, newspapers, and books, or in a sense inscribed in the layout of towns or buildings. I enjoyed doing the research for my most recent novel, *The River Gods*, which is historical fiction. At first, I got too caught up in it, and an early draft of the novel contained about one hundred pages of fairly straight, undigested language other people used to describe emotions and events from the past of this small Massachusetts town. Eventually, I either eliminated these sections or rewrote them considerably, turning their words into someone else's voice or putting together two or three distinct voices from different periods to make one relatively seamless voice of a moment in time. The philosopher Søren Kierkegaard long ago noticed that life can only be understood retrospectively but has to be lived prospectively. Humans are fascinated by history not because we want to know the past, but because we want to predict the future and because we live facing backwards.

This passage is from the "About Us" section of Lewis Lapham's *Lapham's Quarterly*:

Cicero framed the thought as an aphorism, "Not to know what happened before one was born is always to be a child." Children unfamiliar with the world in time make easy marks for the dealers in junk science, totalitarian politics, and quack religion. The general states of amnesia cannot sustain the promise of individual freedom or the practice of democratic self-government. A knowledge of history arms us with our best weapon against the will to ignorance and the joys of superstition, makes possible the revolt against what G.K.

Chesterton once called "the arrogant oligarchy of those who merely happen to be walking about."

Field Maloney, in his obituary of the novelist and historian Shelby Foote, in *Slate*, quoted Foote on what happened when General George McClellan met the general he was replacing, Winfield Scott, at the beginning of the Civil War (Maloney says, "Scott has just been unceremoniously relieved of command of the Union Army by Abraham Lincoln, and he's been replaced by his former deputy, the young dandy George McClellan"). Here is what Foote saw in the encounter between these two important historical figures at a train depot:

> McClellan returned to his quarters and his bed. Rising for the second time that morning, he found his mind so impressed by the farewell at the depot a few hours ago that he took time to describe it in a letter to his wife. After forwarding Scott's greetings to her and the new baby, he philosophized on what he had seen. "The sight of this morning was a lesson to me which I hope not soon to forget. I saw there the end of a long, active, and industrious life, the end of the career of the first soldier; and it was a feeble old man scarce able to walk; hardly anyone there to see him off but his successor. Should I ever become vainglorious and ambitious, remind me of that spectacle."

Shelby Foote takes a novelist's license, in a sense, but he is also simply reporting from a letter McClellan wrote to his wife.

Historians bristle at the idea that they're writing anything remotely like fiction. I asked a colleague of mine in the history department at the University of Denver if she ever read historical fiction. We were about to enter a graduate student's dissertation defense in creative writing (the student's work was historical fiction). My colleague said no. She saw no purpose for historical fiction.

THE STORY OF A YEAR. Read Edward Tannenbaum's book *1900*, Ann Hagedorn's *Savage Peace* (about the year 1919), David Pietrusza's *The Year of the Six Presidents* (about 1920), or Ross Gregory's *A Nation at the Crossroads* (1941). Or find another book that gives you deep insight into a very restricted period of time. You don't have to read the whole book. Browse, pick and choose interesting anecdotes. You are not a college student in a history class (even if you are). You don't have any responsibility to these books or this information. What you're looking for is inspiration, details, fragments, pleasures. Write a piece of fiction that takes place in a small part of one of these years. 750 words.

139

AFTER AUSCHWITZ. Write a short scene set in a Nazi concentration camp. The idea of trying to imagine oneself into such a place or situation is abhorrent. Many have argued over the years that no one has the right to write about the death camps without actual experience of them. The philosopher T.W. Adorno said that writing poetry after Auschwitz was barbaric. The word *barbaric* means uncivilized. I'm all for trying the uncivilized.

Another simple instruction for this exercise is to use the names a handful of people you love as characters in this story. These names should not *be* the people you love; only use their names, not their characteristics or souls. But putting just the names of your loved ones in such horrifying circumstances will be a useful narrative operation. It will be hard to be carefree about this investigation with your own family names involved. 500 words.

THERE IS A TENDENCY among young writers to go slumming (to visit slums for prurient reasons). We want our experience to have been more exotic, dangerous, dirty, and difficult than we think it was. This exercise should be a cure for that kind of desire. It will be no fun. Do some research, which is going to be agonizing. Read Primo Levi's great book *Survival in Auschwitz*. Don't skim this book—read it all. Read histories, too, but I suspect firsthand accounts will be more overwhelming and make it all the more difficult to inhabit the voice of someone surviving this particular death camp.

— 140)

EUNUCH. Imagine a brief snippet of the reality of a eunuch in a harem in Istanbul in 1605. This is a very concrete request of mine, but I also hope you'll take liberties with the suggestion—or not worry too much about being historically accurate. One can write historical fiction that needs no research at all. Here, the problem is not accuracy but imagining one's way into a physical condition. A *eunuch* is a castrated man who is incapable of vaginal intercourse with women for a variety of reasons. The word meant, originally, having charge of a bed, or bed-keeper.

A man writing this piece will obviously feel differently than a woman writing it. 500 words.

MEN WERE CASTRATED for a couple of reasons before the twentieth century—to keep their voices high (for singing), for punishment, subjugation, or enslavement. This is a very particular problem I'm proposing you write about. I don't believe you will necessarily be interested in it, per se, but the idea is to get you to watch the process of exploring some idiosyncratic piece of history and see for yourself how this invigorates your own fiction and desires to recreate history.

Ancient history is full of stuff like this. Castration, slavery, mass murder, female circumcision (well, that's not so ancient).

141

THE DUST BOWL. In parts of Kansas, Nebraska, and Colorado, on April 14, 1935, the worst dust storm in the twentieth century completely blacked out the sun. People died of dust pneumonia. Cows had nothing but dirt in their stomachs and went blind from the dust. Static electricity was so bad before these storms that people stopped shaking hands. Blue flashes of electricity exploded on metal fences. Write a short scene that imagines three people in this dust storm. 500 words.

AGAIN, THIS IS A VERY SPECIFIC historical problem I'm assigning. I've done all the research you need to do in the first four sentences above. Study them very carefully. Rewrite them yourself several times so they become your own thoughts. Add to each sentence a bit of your own idiosyncratic detail, or add a few sentences between the original five.

— **142** —

HISTORY & FICTION. Write a short encounter between a well-known historical figure and a completely fictional character you've already made up in an earlier story of yours. 500 words.

MY STUDENTS HAVE OFTEN EXPRESSED discomfort at the notion of historical figures and fictional figures intermingling in a story. If you're going to write historical fiction, just stick to what's known, they say. If not, write fiction. I defend the writers I've taught who do wonderful things with both fictional and historical characters stepping on to the same stage. The very act of creating a fictional reality that can fit a historical figure means you're fictionalizing.

— **143** —

HISTORY AS LITERARY LOOTING. Write a deliberately false version of a well-known historical event, but add in enough accurate detail to confuse your readers into thinking what you're revealing to them is true. 750 words.

GEORGE WILL, IN A *WASHINGTON POST* COLUMN, wrote this about the films *United 93* and *JFK*:

> [Paul] Greengrass's scrupulosity is evident in the movie's conscientious, minimal, and minimally speculative departures from the facts about the flight painstakingly assembled for the Sept. 11 commission report. This is emphatically not a "docudrama" like Oliver Stone's execrable *JFK*, which was "history" as a form

of literary looting in which the filmmaker used just enough facts to lend a patina of specious authenticity to tendentious political ax-grinding.

Donald Barthelme, from his amazing little story "Paraguay":

A government error resulting in the death of a statistically insignificant portion of the population (less than one-fortieth of 1 percent) has made people uneasy. A skelp of questions and answers is fused at high temperature (1400° C) and then passed through a series of protracted caresses. Amelioration of the condition results. Paraguay is not old. It is new, a new country. Rough sketches suggest its "look." Heavy yellow drops like pancake batter fall from its sky. I held a bouquet of umbrellas in each hand.

George Will's annoyance with Oliver Stone's movie and Donald Barthelme's pure fiction of an actual place may seem light years apart in terms of sensibility. But there is a common thread. Will says that writers and filmmakers should not bother to do history unless they are relentlessly accurate. Barthelme says, "What is accurate? What is truth? What is history?" In this exercise, I want you to play with this notion of fiction and history. When it comes down to it, what is history on the minute level? A letter Abraham Lincoln wrote to one of his generals outlining strategy for an upcoming battle in the Civil War may seem incontrovertible truth and fact, but what if Lincoln was writing to a general he distrusted? What if he could not give him accurate details of the battle plans for the other generals in the area for fear this one general would petulantly try to outshine these other rivals? History is an educated guess as often as it is a hard look at historical fact.

_____ 144)_____

CHRISTMAS EVERY THREE MONTHS. This is an exercise for people over forty. Write an incomplete short story about how time, in one's middle age, seems to speed up a great deal. By necessity, this story fragment will be a summary, not a description of individual scenes or conversations. 500 words.

FRAN LEIBOWITZ SAID, "After forty, Christmas seems to arrive every three months." I am fifty-one as I type this sentence. I am endlessly surprised, this last decade or so, by how quickly time passes, how clearly I see the arc of friends' lives and my own life, how familiar experience is that happened ten years ago is (but how unfamiliar it is from two days past or twenty years past).

_____ 145)_____

CBGB. What is it about places like CBGB, the bar in the East Village in New York that showcased the early punk rock scene in the 1970s? Think of your own significant place, like this grungy bar (it was grungy in 1978 and still grungy when it closed in 2006). Or just write about CBGB. Do some research into whichever place you choose to write about. The place doesn't have to be famous—it can be important only to you and the friends of your youth (or your parents' youth). Imagine your way into one of these sites of happening. 750 words.

JIM FARBER, IN THE NEW YORK *DAILY NEWS*, on the closing of CBGB:

> Like many, I first read about a new scene percolating at the place
> where Bleecker Street slams into the Bowery in a 1974 *Village Voice*
> article by the wonderful James Wolcott. I was sixteen and so hob-
> bled with just a learner's driving permit. By the time '74 turned to
> '75, however, I had the necessary license to begin tooling my 1969
> Chevy Nova down to one of the dankest intersections in the city.
> Braving the squeegee men, robbers, and ne'er-do-wells who ran
> the area at the time, I arrived with two friends in early '75 to see a
> band whimsically titled Talking Heads. At the time, they were then
> a spindly, acoustic trio. "Psycho Killer" was their signature piece,
> and it sounded funnier, darker, and more wondrously odd than any-
> thing I'd heard up until that point. Soon, we saw the Ramones, who
> played faster and shorter than anyone had in history, Blondie, who
> brilliantly turned girl pop into punk, and Television, who found an
> impossible intersection between The Velvet Underground and the
> Grateful Dead.
>
> Because I was still in high school, I took the genius of all this
> for granted. Having idealized Manhattan as Oz, I thought that, natu-
> rally, one comes to the city and everything is brilliant.

I lived around the corner from CBGB in the winter of 1978, when I shared
an apartment with my brother for a quarter of my senior year of college (I
had an internship at Viking Press). We used to get phone calls for CBGB
because our number was one digit different than theirs. I began to call
the bar on Fridays to find out who was playing, because it was easier to

just give out the information than to try to explain to the generally stoned callers that they had not reached CBGB. I never went to the place, even though I knew it was a mecca for a new kind of rock music. I am deaf in one ear, so I've always been protective of my hearing in my good ear, and rock bars are not pleasant for me. But I do wish I'd taken a look at the history happening around the corner from me that winter.

CHARACTER VS. CARICATURE

On the subject of how to make a character in fiction, James Wood quotes Ford Madox Ford quoting a sentence from Guy de Maupassant: "He was a gentleman with red whiskers who always went first through a doorway." This simple action suggests a bully, a self-involved (as opposed to self-made) man, or perhaps simply a man always in a hurry. The word *caricature* meant originally a satirical picture or cartoon, from another similar verb that means to load or exaggerate. *Character*, on the other hand, comes from the word for engraved mark. Eventually the meaning of the word was extended to include *a defining quality*. So a caricature is an exaggeration and a character is a person's defining quality.

————————————— **146**)—————————————

A PROSPERO FIGURE. Write a prosy outline or a rough sketch for a short story. In this sketch, fiddle with the idea of one female character who knows more than the rest of the characters. This shouldn't be magical or supernatural. This person simply has a better view of what is going on around her than anyone else. She is able, with this foreknowledge of her friends' actions, to gently manipulate them to act slightly or significantly different than they would have without her unseen help. 250 words.

IN SHAKESPEARE'S PLAY *The Tempest*, Prospero is a nobleman who is exiled to an island full of magic and spirits. Prospero learns to harness this magic for his own needs and desires by means of his own learnedness and great library. When the men who caused him to be shipwrecked on the island pass near it, he causes a tempest to shipwreck them as well. *The Tempest* is generally accepted as Shakespeare's last play, and Prospero is thought to represent the playwright himself. At the end of the play, Prospero renounces his magic, a parallel to the plays Shakespeare wrote. Here are the first two lines of Prospero's epilogue:

> Now my charms are all o'erthrown,
> And what strength I have's mine own

By *a Prospero figure* I mean a character in a story who seems to be observing the story itself, to a certain extent, and who manipulates other characters in the story to bend to his will, often for the good of others. Some examples of modern Prospero figures are Thomas Crown in *The Thomas Crown Affair* (particularly the more recent version) or Cary Grant's character C.K. Dexter Haven in *The Philadelphia Story*. Both characters exhibit a winking, self-satisfied attitude, as if they were just a bit ahead of the plot.

147

WALLACE & GROMIT. Write a short sequence of scenes about two human characters. One of these people speaks; the other does not speak at all. The nontalker can speak, but chooses not to, or perhaps the talkative one speaks so much the nontalker can't get a word in edgewise. These two characters are constant companions. The talker is not in the least put out by the silence of his pal. 750 words.

GROMIT OF *WALLACE & GROMIT* is the dog of this series of Claymation cartoons. He is the completely silent one, the savior of nearly every scrape

Wallace gets himself into. Gromit is more than just a silent "actor." He is a force, despite, or perhaps because of, his silence. There are other modern-day silent partners: (Jay and) Silent Bob, (Penn and) Teller. Gromit stands out from this group because he can't speak. He is a dog, after all. The whole premise of this wonderful show is that the dog gets the human out of trouble. He may not be able to speak, but he can drive a truck, fly a plane, handle the intricate machines Wallace invents, and tend his own garden with loving care. There is an exercise in *The 3 A.M. Epiphany* similar to this one, Silent Partner. In that exercise I suggest that you have one quiet person in a group of people. The difference here is that these two are a unit, and the silent one is nearly always silent, while the talker does nearly all the talking.

148

FLÂNEUR. Write about an idle man-about-town, a lounger, or a saunterer (of course you can also make this a woman-about-town). Walter Benjamin liked this word, *flâneur,* and he used it to describe many of Charles Baudelaire's and Edgar Allan Poe's characters, particularly the narrator of Poe's story "The Man of the Crowd." A lounger nowadays does not have much cachet. You might call bloggers modern-day *flâneurs.* But a real city observer, a person who does nothing but study the behaviors or gestures of passers-by on the street, for hours at a time, would be an interesting figure to hang a story on. Most contemporary American cities are not conducive to *flâneurs*—they demand automobiles. New York and San Francisco alone, perhaps, allow a person on the street to observe many strangers at many different socioeconomic levels. But you could modify this notion of an urbane observer of the world—have your *flâneur* go to a mall during the Christmas rush, or a baseball game, or a large friendly park on a warm summer day. 750 words.

EUROPEANS TO THIS DAY like to stroll around central parts of their cities, watching and being watched (each as important as the other). In the United States we tend to do this in cars. Think of *American Graffiti* or any number of other American films that show this rite of adolescent passage. I practiced my apprenticeship as a young writer in Seattle, where I lived for four years after college in Minnesota (from 1978 to 1982). I did a great deal of lounging around outdoors or in public places. I rode buses all over the city, with a notebook, listening to conversations, observing human encounters, categorizing behaviors. I once went out to the airport and sat along with other family and friends awaiting the flights of loved ones. This was a more innocent time; someone without a ticket could actually go to the gate. I was startled by my access to these intimate, emotional encounters. Occasionally, my neighbors would notice me writing in my journal and come to some sort of private conclusion about what I was doing, but no one ever asked me to stop.

———————————— **149** ————————————

A BEAUTIFUL WOMAN. Describe a couple of encounters a beautiful woman has with several strangers within a short space of time—an hour or two. Don't tell us directly that this is a beautiful woman, the sort of beautiful woman who turns heads, who receives slightly better treatment—and higher pay—than the average human being. Will she be untroubled by her beauty? Does she occasionally dress down to avoid the attention? Would she use her appearance sometimes for advantage? 500 words.

LISTEN TO HOW THIS THOUGHT (from a character in the TV series *Battlestar Galactica*) describes self-possession without showing us anything about the woman's beauty: "She had a way of walking, processional, as if on the way to her own execution."

Why not do an exercise about a beautiful man? You could certainly change the rules for this exercise and do that. Beautiful men don't provoke quite the same quality of head turning. But I'm a man, so I may not be the best judge of that issue.

— 150 —

THE FICTION WRITER & THE LAWYER. Write a brief scene with a lawyer and a fiction writer. Trial lawyers are professional storytellers, but they spend 98 percent of their time going over fine print. Corporate lawyers are professional researchers who look for threads and stories among the thousands of documents they study. A writer might know a good lawyer joke, like the one about the fence that borders Heaven and Hell. (The steering committee in Hell sends a letter to Heaven saying, after much study, their lawyers feel the fence is Heaven's property and therefore the repairs are Heaven's responsibility. Heaven replies that since they have no lawyers, they accept the responsibility.)

A writer in his early twenties, who has not had any success, and his high school classmate who's just graduated from law school, will have quite varying views of the world, but their childhood bonds may overcome those differences. A successful writer in her thirties and her corporate lawyer sister may be unable to see anything with the same set of eyes, yet they may still love one another as if it were a competition to see who loves the other better. 500 words.

EDMUND BURKE SAID the study of law sharpens the mind by narrowing it. Robert Benchley said, "It took me fifteen years to discover that I had no talent for writing, but I couldn't give it up because by that time I was too famous." The Roman rhetorician Quintilian said, "A liar needs a good memory." *New York Times* columnist Maureen Dowd took a break from her column in 2005 to write an odd travel story, "In Cancún, Girls Gone Mild." She is neither a fiction writer nor a lawyer, but I like how she views herself and the man (who may have been a lawyer) at the end of the paragraph below. She also speaks of herself as if she were still a twenty-something who took "spring breaks," when in fact she's a beautiful, tart, insightful, and mean-spirited fifty-something political observer (her critiques of Hillary Clinton are very unfair, but her equally savage devastations of George W. Bush have almost made up for the Clinton-bashing, at least in my mind):

> My spring break experiences were grisly. One year I went to San Juan, where a young Puerto Rican businessman I met at a cockfight tried to insist that I give him sexual favors because he once dated a girl who dated Elvis, and where my roommate and I got kicked out of a bar at gunpoint because some *señoritas de la noche* thought we were encroaching on their territory. Another year we went to Tampa.

It was so awful that my only memory is of a local guy complaining to his friends about me: "You tell this girl dirt's brown, she's gonna argue with ya."

151

AMBITION. Write a fragment of fiction about a central character in his early twenties who is very ambitious. What sort of ambition? This could be a budding scientist, a snowboarder, a painter, a lawyer, or a candlestick maker. The fierce, driving ambition of this character is your main concern. How does this obvious ambition affect this person's friends or family? Do all applaud it? Do some find it annoying or intimidating? Are some dismayed by it because they think this person can't possibly succeed at these ambitions? 500 words.

WHAT IS AMBITION? The *Oxford English Dictionary*'s modern definition is the ardent desire to rise to high position or to attain rank, influence, or distinction. Is a person with great ambition pleasant or unpleasant? If the object of ambition for this character is ridiculous, the character is ridiculous, but if this person could succeed at achieving these ambitions, the character is noble and interesting. My friend Don Berger gave me some very simple advice about my fiction in 1981. He said, "You should be more ambitious." I replied that I wasn't all that ambitious, but immediately I questioned my answer and began to rethink my ambitions as a writer. I *was* ambitious, and it struck me that one had to make this simple decision, to take on large subjects, to become the better and better writer one has to will oneself to become. No one else is going to do it for you.

—————————————— 152) ——————————————

SELF-LOATHING. Write an incomplete piece of narrative in the third person and imagine an attached third-person narrator who despises herself. The fact that this observer of the narrative hates herself is inconsequential to whatever story you tell. But make it very plain that this person is self-loathing. 500 words.

AN EXERCISE OF THIS SORT might seem to be in the vein of unreliable narrations, a common tactic. I want you to make this person perfectly trustworthy (or mostly honest about the story being told). The fact that this person has so little self-love does not mean we can't believe the story he tells.

On November 5, 2006, Ted Haggard wrote a letter to the New Life Church he founded. In the letter he explained his sins (homosexuality and consorting with a male prostitute) and the reasons he was being fired. "There is a part of my life that is so repulsive and dark," he said, "that I've been warring against it all of my adult life ... The public person I was wasn't a lie; it was just incomplete. When I stopped communicating about my problems, the darkness increased and finally dominated me." We have many examples of this sort of hypocrisy and self-loathing, from Jim Bakker to Eliot Spitzer.

—————————————— 153) ——————————————

CLOSE TALKER. Write a fragment of fiction from the point of view of a character that stands too close to other people in conversation. The character you explore violates personal space—which is usually about six feet, in the United States. Your close talker is aware of violating other people's personal space. Let your close talker use the discomfort to his advantage somehow. Do not make this character pathetic or foolish. 500 words.

UNDERSTANDING THE IDEA of proprioception might be useful in this exercise. Proprioception is the physical knowledge of where parts of the body are in relation to each other. Hold your hand behind your back and wave it around. Most people can visualize the shape of this hand wave. Some people lack this skill, and perhaps close talkers do, too. In the sitcom *Seinfeld*, Elaine has a boyfriend who is a close talker who adores Jerry's parents, who are in New York for a visit. He exhibits two inappropriate behaviors—close talking and excessive love of a girlfriend's ex-boyfriend's parents.

154

COSTUMES. Put a character you already know well in a costume and let the reader see this character morph into another character. Actors pick up a single prop and they become something or someone else. Regular folk put on a costume, especially when a mask is part of the costume, and they also easily become someone else. 600 words.

"I PRETENDED TO BE SOMEBODY I wanted to be and I finally became that person," Cary Grant said. "Or he became me. Or we met at some point." Costumes and disguises are often simply reflections of who we will become at some point in our lives.

──────── **155** ────────

FRUITFULNESS I. KIPPERS. Use six or eight of the names below in an imitation of an office memo. In the memo, these named people should be assigned duties that have something to do (however bizarrely) with these names. Take this very strange set of names seriously. 500 words.

MY FRIEND SHAWN HUELLE once posted a list of names of "people" who sent him mail (read: spam) on his blog rocket2nowhere.com. I've captured just the first thirty of these names:

> Gangrene Q. Surplice, Currycombs K. Pursued, Gearboxes S. Tasmania, Freemason A. Implausible, Miter L. Anesthetic, Keyword D. Detonate, Drunker U. Myopia, Monoxide S. Prokofiev, Grope E. Virgo, Ostracism K. Matted, Patriarchs D. Juvenile, Respectables C. Modulates, Discomfited G. Troyes, Turfing T. Debauchery, Esmerelda B. Slothing, Luxurient P. Bent, Milliner H. Maunder, Audacity T. Hurl, Generates I. Garrison, Sprees M. Saturnalia, Limpidity J. Vibrates, Giraffes D. Possible, Fruitfulness I. Kippers, Woven C. Pleasurably, Syndrome C. Disapproval, Bellwether G. Cursed, Rehabs U. Ostrich, Hinged T. Rupture, Apollo A. Homebodies, or Sugary P. Dunlap.

──────── **156** ────────

REJUVENILES. Write a fragment of fiction in which one of the main characters is an adult over twenty-five years of age who lives at home, perhaps not in his parents' basement, and maybe not permanently, but nevertheless is back in the bosom of the family.

I spent a summer at my parents' house in 1987, before I went to teach at the American University in Cairo that fall. I'd been living in New York, and my apartment sublet was not available after June 1. The summer seemed like a good idea, beforehand. I was trying to finish up my first novel, *Still Life With Insects*, and I was doing some last editorial work for a New York publisher so I could reasonably leave the city. I was thirty. I'd been on my own since the age of eighteen. I thought of myself as an adult. My mother especially did not seem to share this blithe assessment of myself, even though I had a good job looming on the horizon and would be out of the country for at least two years. 750 words.

CHRISTOPHER NOXON, in the *New York Times*, wrote about a type of people he called rejuveniles, "adults who act and think more like kids than conventional adults."

> These are the not-quite-grown-ups ... who delay marriage and parenthood, the better to maintain lives of fun and flexibility, who then bond and play with their own offspring in ways their parents would find ridiculous, and whose consumer choices have expanded the market for everything from micromini cars to gourmet cupcakes.

Noxon is the author of *Rejuvenile: Kickball, Cartoons, Cupcakes, and the Reinvention of the American Grown-up.*

VOICES & TALK

Voice casting is a common credit one sees at the end of movies. I don't know what that means, but I've heard that in the editing phase of movies, filmmakers often look around for good additional voices and sound effects to throw into scenes to add depth and complexity. When I listen to a 1930s film, one thing I'm struck by is how silent the film is sometimes. A character walks down a hotel hallway, and I hear nothing, not even footsteps on the floor. By the late twentieth century sound had become much more dense and layered in film. You can pick out many different effects and vocal talents at work around the edges of these movies. This is something of the equivalent of three dimensions in sound. If there were such a thing as voice casting in fiction, it would be to capture the essential quality of a character—your narrator, of course, but also the many major and minor characters in the book or story. Each voice should be recognizable and unique.

———————————— **157** ————————————

A BURGLAR SMOKING A FINE CIGAR. Look at the handful of descriptions of famous people's voices below. Think about this problem for a while—listen to someone on TV and don't look at the image on the screen. Write down the images that spring to mind when you hear this well-known voice. Collect a list of these phrases. Then think of someone you know well personally. If you have a tape recording (or a voice mail) of a friend or family member with a distinctive style, do the same thing. Write up comparisons this person's voice evokes. It does not matter if you're accurate. You're not looking to be correct—you're looking for vivid word pictures you can use.

When you've got enough of these phrases to play with, write a short fragment of a scene in which a person (your listener) overhears another person in the next room talking about something important and compelling. This person is speaking to someone else (or more than one other person), but give us only the monologue. Use a few of these phrases you've collected. Devote most of the energy of this production to this monologue, not to the listener or much of anything else. 500 words.

MICHAEL MODE TOLD NPR's Brian McConnachie that the sound of Jack Nicholson's voice is like "awakening in the middle of the night to the smell of a fine cigar being smoked by a burglar robbing your house." Here are some other vocal impressions listeners wrote in to McConnachie with: Truman Capote sounds like "eggnog with too much whiskey," according to Susan Surota. Ken Bolinsky compares Marilyn Monroe's voice to "the steam rising from a soufflé." The general impressions of Morgan Freeman's voice are "front porches, rocking chairs, brandy, sandpaper, the fireside, walnuts, grandfathers, and the voice of our conscience."

——————————————— **158** ———————————————

FRACTURED FAIRY TALE. Write a short piece of fiction in the distinctive voice of an actor or a person you know. This is much more complex than it sounds. I'm thinking particularly of Edward Everett Horton (1886–1970), the actor in *Top Hat* with Fred Astaire and *Holiday* with Katharine Hepburn and Cary Grant—with his wonderful warbling voice, which Jay Ward used to great effect in the Rocky and Bullwinkle secondary cartoon *Fractured Fairy Tales.* Go to YouTube and type in the phrase *Fractured Fairy Tales*, and you'll find a half-dozen examples. Horton's voice acted as a sweet but petulant omniscient narrator following the action, commenting on it, sometimes interfering with the characters that were in the midst of the action. The idea of this exercise is to use this voice in our heads to tell a story that has nothing to do with the voice, to see what happens when we try to channel another voice than our own to tell a piece of fiction. 750 words.

— **159** —

PLANTS. Restaurants sometimes hire people to stand in line at their establishments and speak loudly to each other about how good the food is. This is a form of advertising, though it seems a bit unfair—well, what advertising plays fair? Write a short scene with six or eight people in it. Put two "plants" in the scene. You could go with this notion of a restaurant line, but you could also go in another direction. The "plants" could be doing something unsinister like subliminal advertising or they could be corporate spies. They could also be urban anthropologists studying their subjects on-site (urban or social anthropology often practices participant observation—American ethnographers studying American urban life in some specific fashion). Never tell us who the spies are and who the subjects of this "study" are. 750 words.

— **160** —

UNBELIEVING. Two characters are talking. One keeps saying, "I don't believe a word you're saying," or something to that effect. This first character indeed does not believe anything the second character says, but the two nevertheless carry on a conversation as if a collection of truths were piling up behind them, in the past. And if the first character does not believe a word the second character is saying, what we have is another layer of fiction below the fiction you're trying to propose. The first character is either telling lies, or the second character is incapable of believing the truths the first character is speaking. 500 words.

THIS IS WHAT ESSENTIALLY happens between reader and writer. If the reader keeps saying, "I don't believe a word you're saying" to the writer, the writer is in trouble. Or it is possible the writer wants the reader to react this way, with disbelief. Remember, the most convincing truth a fiction can convey is often delivered by a terribly unreliable narrator. We don't believe the lies, but we do tend to trust what the narrator is *not* saying.

---161)---

TRIALOGUE. Carefully write a conversation between three people, giving each person equal weight in the talk. In its early Greek use, *dialogue* meant to speak alternately. This alternation of speech—perhaps a rigidly observed order and length of speech—is what I'm looking for in this trialogue. A similar word, to *converse*, from which we get conversation, originally meant to pass one's life or dwell with. The Latin word *conversare* literally meant to turn oneself about, pass one's life, abide, live somewhere, or keep company with. The transference of sense from "live with" to "talk with" is recent in French and English. It is important to keep this notion of living with and talking with someone. 500 words.

—————— **162**)——————

A CAR WRECK IN REPOSE (a line from James Wolcott). Write a short scene that takes place entirely inside a vehicle that has been in a serious accident. Let there be a driver and two passengers. All are badly injured, but all are conscious. They cannot escape from the vehicle, but the vehicle is not about to explode. Still, things aren't good. Write about their perceptions and their fractured conversation in the moments before the ambulance arrives. 500 words.

—————— **163**)——————

THERAPEUTIC LYING. Imagine a situation in which one of your already familiar characters feels she has no choice but to indulge in therapeutic lying, which is explained below. 500 words.

RANDY COHEN, THE ETHICIST for the *New York Times*, wrote an answer to a question posed by a reader from Florida:

> Before her recent death, my mother lived in a nursing facility. She said often and wistfully that she wanted to go home, which was unlikely to happen. She could not walk without assistance and was no longer capable of living independently. The nurses told her that she could go home when she got stronger, calling this "therapeutic lying." They said that without it, she would have had no hope and nothing to live for. Were these lies ethical? —*K.B., Tallahassee, Fla.*

They were not. Deliberately misleading a patient robs her of her dignity. This is not to suggest that nurses should deal harshly with patients, but that tact and sensitivity are preferable to outright falsehood. Instead of saying: "Your condition is hopeless," the nurses can say, "Wouldn't it be great if you could go home?" or "You'll feel better if you come to therapy." That is, encourage a patient, humor a patient, but do not lie. The benefits of deceit might flow less to a patient than to the nurses. It can be tough to care for someone who holds no hope, and such lies can encourage an otherwise reluctant patient to participate in physical therapy or take necessary medication. But the short-term benefit of jollying a patient along with false hope does not offset the long-term peril of lying. Sooner or later many patients figure out what's what, and those who have been lied to may well resent it. Practitioners do better to deal honestly even with reluctant patients from the get-go. Practicality aside, being old and infirm should not deprive a person of being treated honorably and respectfully. It may be that someone in your mother's circumstances could go home. Dr. Michele Barry, who teaches medicine at Yale University, told me, "There is a home hospice program that can actually honor these wishes for folks even with noncancerous but terminal conditions along with home health aides." When the situation allows, it is a compassionate and ethical solution.

164

DONALD RUMSFELD. The former Secretary of Defense said this at a press conference, some time in the months after the beginning of the Iraq War in 2003:

As we know, there are known knowns; there are things we know we know. We also know there are known unknowns; that is to say we know there are some things we do not know. But there are also unknown unknowns, the ones we don't know we don't know.

Use this found poetry of the former Secretary of Defense as the scaffolding of a very short story. Found poetry is language taken from other sources and relined to look like poetry. Let the philosophy (or the political undercurrent) of the three sentences act as the hidden philosophy of your story. Use as many of the words, and even the proper repetition of the words, as you can. Your main goal in this exercise is to maintain the strangely jaunty voice of Donald Rumsfeld throughout your prose. 500 words.

─────────────────(**165**)─────────────────

DRESSING UP. Women spend three years of their lives dressing to go out. Write a short scene in which a woman is getting dressed for an evening out. Her man has finished dressing long ago. He is called upon to "help" her decide which clothes or jewelry to wear. She is certain of her taste in such things, but she also enjoys the input of this man. The attention in the conversation is broken—between the clothes and jewelry being tried on and any other subject you want to explore. 500 words.

WOMEN'S EMPATHY IS GREATER than men's. But women are not as good at systematizing. Men on average are more interested in how things work than women. They enjoy systems, and they are less interested in talking about emotional problems. The complex world of women's clothing—all the accoutrements, the color combinations, the sparkles, and the choices between accentuating the body and hiding it—is one system straight men rarely have interest in or understanding of. The conversation men and women are likely to have is going to be strained. A woman is not likely to empathize with her man's avoidance of this duty—to help her fluff up for an evening out.

FAMILY & FRIENDS

Our family and our closest friends form a community unlike any other we belong to. These people often serve as models for the fictional characters we create, whether they want to or not. It is worth thinking deeply about these nearly mythological figures in our lives. Lately, in my fiction, I have stopped using other names for my own family when they appear in my novels. I use the names Brian Kiteley, Geoffrey Kiteley, Barbara Kiteley (now Hill), Murray Kiteley, and Jean Kiteley. I have lost the urge to find other names for these people.

In *Still Life With Insects*, I did enjoy renaming my family. My brother became Humphrey, because of Lyndon Johnson's vice president, Hubert Humphrey, whom my brother somewhat reluctantly supported for president in 1968 when his true favorite, Johnson, dropped out of the race (Geoff was twelve and in rebellion against my Eugene McCarthy-supporting parents). Explore your own family history and the way this small or large group works, and you may find all you can know about the rest of the population of the world.

—————————————(**166**)——————————————

PARENTS AS TWO CONTINENTS. Write about your own parents in essay format. Tell us what they might have been before they met, and what has become of them after their marriage (or divorce). Don't describe them as individuals (even if they divorced). Keep the tone neutral, if you can. Maintain the voice of a calm, witty essay until you've written about 300 words. Then slowly turn this essay into a brief story of an intriguing scene that involves both your parents and you. Don't describe a fight. Keep the calm essay-writer voice as you turn toward narrative. 750 words.

My FIRST MFA WORKSHOP teacher, Mark Mirsky, listened to my initial story in his workshop that fall of 1982, and he seemed impressed. He said, "Who the hell is this guy?"

I'd submitted with my application to the program some of a novel I was working on, a political thriller about a sabotage of the Indian Point nuclear power plant fifty miles north of New York City. Mark had not been impressed by this writing, and he was somewhat more intrigued by the story I'd written about my brother in Spain in 1969, which was what I submitted for that first workshop. Mark asked me to come to his office for a chat a few days later, and he started lobbing questions at me about the thriller and my own history. Where was I from? Who and what was my father? When he heard I was from Northampton, Massachusetts, and that my father was a philosopher, he said, "You're an idiot for not writing about that stuff."

Mark was the son of an intimidating judge near Boston. He felt that Kafka had it right—all writing should start with the father. He did not like my story (and a later story) about my gay brother. "It's a waste of your energy," he said. He urged me to explore more important history than baby steps toward a meek understanding of a pathetic sinful nature (Mark had recently rediscovered his own Judaism and he was a startlingly puritanical man).

I disagreed with Mark, but I also listened, and slowly I began to piece together stories about the rest of my family. I could not write about my father, in part because I found his analytic philosophy so difficult. I had very little education in philosophy, but I struggled through the essentials of this Anglo-American analytic philosophy, and I learned slowly that I was drawn to another character in my family tree, my grandfather, my father's father, who collected beetles. I liked him not because of his writings (or only indirectly) or his mind, but because of his voice. He and I were very much alike and we had similar senses of humor. He was also someone I loved unconditionally (my father, as sweet and smart as he was, caused a complex array of emotions in me, not all of them happy). The moment I began writing in my grandfather's voice, I realized I'd found a way of writing that worked, whereas everything else I'd done before was just fiction.

167

THANKSGIVINGS. Write a short piece of fiction that summarizes four consecutive Thanksgivings at home with adult children, parents, in-laws, and stray friends brought in from the cold. Do not give us a capsule of each Thanksgiving, one after another. Mix and match details from all four meals. In other words, mess up the time sequence. 750 words.

JOSEPH EPSTEIN, in a *Wall Street Journal* editorial, talks a bit about the best American holiday:

> Thanksgiving is not about children. It remains resolutely an adult holiday about grown-up food and drink and football. The weather, which provides the backdrop to Thanksgiving, is also much in its favor. In most parts of the country cool, sometimes cold, it doesn't usually blow the holiday away with tornados, hurricanes, or great snowstorms. Warm jackets, sweaters, corduroy trousers are the order of the day—comfort clothes, the sartorial equivalent of comfort food. Comfort food is what Thanksgiving provides, and to the highest possible power. Large browned turkeys, rich heavy stuffings, sweet potatoes, cranberries.

Thanksgivings at my home, throughout my life, were dominated by five cooks. My father's mother Elsie was the first, my father the second, my brother, who became a chef at a good Italian restaurant in New York the last decade of his life, and then my sister Barbara and my wife Cynthia. I've always enjoyed Thanksgiving for all the reasons Epstein gives. I recall gales of laughter over the meal when I was a kid and into adulthood. There were also great stresses—family and illness. On my brother's last Thanksgiving, for which Cynthia and I returned to Northampton from Ohio, he went into the hospital. He never left the hospital, and he died on Christmas Eve a month later. Still, I remember that Thanksgiving, at my sister's house in Newburyport, Massachusetts, as a very festive, even cheerful time.

————————————————————— **168** —————————————————————

BROTHERS. Write a couple of fragments of narrative about two brothers who have witnessed a terrible automobile accident. Only one of the five occupants of the cars has survived. The brothers can do nothing to help, but they have to stick around as witnesses. They were on foot, at the intersection in a medium-sized American city, and they had the best view of any of the other nearby pedestrians of the two cars colliding. Keep off to the side with the brothers. Don't pay an awful lot of attention to this accident. Use the gaps between the fragments to show how much time is passing. 750 words.

THERE IS AN ARMENIAN saying: If brothers were a good thing, God would have a brother. The brothers in your exercise do not have to hate each other, but try to explore their discomfort with each other and their quite different responses to this crisis.

————————————————————— **169** —————————————————————

SISTERS. Write a short short story about two sisters. One of the sisters is the oldest of her family; the other sister is either the youngest or simply younger than the older sister. They do not like each other. They sometimes despise each other. Put these two women in the same situation as the brothers in the previous exercise—witnesses to an awful car crash. Do not end this piece with any kind of reconciliation. Follow the basic rules of *Seinfeld*: no hugs. In fact, don't end the piece, just stop it abruptly. 500 words.

HERE IS A SNIPPET of the Sharon Olds poem, "The Elder Sister," from her collection *The Dead and the Living*:

> When I look at my eldest sister now
> I think how she had to go first, down through the
> birth canal, to force her way
> head-first through the tiny channel,
> the pressure of Mother's muscles on her brain,
> the tight walls scraping her skin.

This is not pretty. Read the rest of the poem, which describes an even more brutal and unhappy relationship: "She protected me ... as a hostage protects the one who makes her escape as I made my escape, with my sister's body held in front of me." The bluntness of these sentiments—the hair-raising details of terrifying sibling rivalry—should be useful. Don't be afraid of this sort of emotion.

170

BIRTH ORDER. Write a fragment of fiction about a three-sibling family. The youngest and the middle children seriously battle the oldest for something. This should be a war of wits, not fists or hair pulling. 500 words.

THE OLDEST CHILDREN are more likely to go to college than the younger children in a family. Older siblings feel that the younger siblings get away with things they were not able to when they were young. The first child believes she must gain superiority over other children. The second child rarely has the parents' complete attention and acts as if life were a race. If the first child is good, the second often becomes bad. The second child develops abilities the first child doesn't have. The youngest child expects others to do things, make decisions, and take responsibility.

This is just a handful of the clichés of birth order. Are they true? It doesn't matter. If you have other siblings, you know your own rules of birth order. Write them down, as if they were official and universal.

ABANDONMENT. Show us the great horror of a child losing one or both parents, from a child's point of view. Have the child observe the moment of separation (either by death or another form of removing the parent). Children's literature is full of terror, abandonment, and violence. Don't be afraid of it, on behalf of the child of your story. Children are much more resilient than we give them credit for. In any event, this is fiction. You're imagining a situation every child fears. 750 words.

ON NPR'S *FRESH AIR*, Terry Gross asked director David Cronenberg what scared him most in movies when he was young. He recalled the scenes in *Dumbo* and *Bambi* where the children were forcibly separated from their parents. Dumbo's mother is not killed, as Bambi's is, but she is locked up and may be lost to the little elephant with the big ears.

— 172)—

CHILD ABUSE. Write a monologue of an adult male (someone over twenty-five years of age) who was badly abused as a child. Do not make this adult a killer or even a sociopath (someone incapable of honest human interactions with others). Do not dwell on this abuse in your monologue, but don't shy away from it either. The character you're developing is hobbled by this abuse, but he has bigger fish to fry. 500 words.

THE FOLLOWING HAUNTING passage is from "Little Miss Sunshine: America's Obsession with JonBenet Ramsey," by James R. Kincaid, in *Slate*:

> Kids really do not fare very well in our culture: Millions of children are, in fact, abused in unspeakable ways. Five hundred thousand kids every year are classified as "throwaways" (children whose parents or guardians will not let them live at home, as distinguished from "runaways"). As many as 800,000 are beaten horribly. Even more are subject to emotional abuse and neglect. How much attention do they get? Instead, we focus our attention, almost all of it, on stranger-danger: things like abductions, of which there are between one hundred and two hundred annually. Our carefully controlled outrage is generated for our own purposes, certainly not to protect the children.

— 173)—

FRIENDSHIPS OF THE GOOD. Write a couple of happy-go-lucky scenes of two very old and good friends. Do not break up this friendship or threaten it in any way. Explore the reasons these two people might indeed be permanent friends, but don't tell us why. Let us see how their friendship operates—on a hike in the mountains; during a walk through a museum; at a sports event both love but don't need to pay a great deal of attention to. 750 words.

IN *NICOMACHEAN ETHICS*, Aristotle talks about friendship. Tim Madigan, in *Philosophy Now*, describes the sturdiest type of friendship:

> Friendships of the good tend to be lifelong, are often formed in childhood or adolescence, and will exist so long as the friends continue to remain virtuous in each other's eyes. To have more than a handful of such friends of the good, Aristotle states, is indeed a fortunate thing. Rare indeed are such friendships, for people of this kind are rare. Or as my mother used to say, "Make new friends but keep the old, for one is silver and the other is gold." Such friendships of the good require time and intimacy—to truly know people's finest qualities you must have deep experiences with them and close connections.

Other types of friendships Aristotle talks of are friendships of utility and friendships of pleasure. Friendships of utility are relationships of convenience, people who are useful to each other. Friends of pleasure delight in one another's company and are most common in one's youth. These friendships are often based on nothing more than the pure desire for friendship itself, for companionship. Both friendships of utility and friendships of pleasure are relatively short-lived, according to Aristotle.

—————————— **174** ——————————

FRIENDSHIP'S END. Write about the end of a friendship. I suggest you do this in such a short space in order to avoid telling us how wonderful—or how awful—the friendship was in the long lead-up to this natural dissolution.

Your job is to give us very efficiently the particulars of a worthy and perhaps once-healthy friendship. But you should also show us why the friendship is ending (or why it has to end). 500 words.

JOSEPH EPSTEIN QUOTES Samuel Johnson on friendship in a piece he wrote for *Commentary*: "It is painful to consider that there is no human possession of which the duration is less certain."

Epstein continues:

Some friendships die on their own, of simple inanition, having been quietly allowed to lapse by the unacknowledged agreement of both parties. Others break down because time has altered old friends, given them different interests, values, points of view. In still others, only one party works at the friendship, while the other belongs to what Truman Capote called (in a letter to the critic Newton Arvin, his ex-lover) "some odd psychological type ... that only writes when he is written to." And then of course there are the friendships that end when one friend betrays or is felt to betray the other, or fails to come through in a crisis, or finds himself violently disputing the other on matters of profoundest principle.

_____ 175)_____

OUR PETS. Write a short fragment of fiction about a beloved family pet that intervenes somehow in a family crisis. Don't do a Lassie story. ("What are you trying to say, girl, that Timmy's fallen down a well?") Treat the animal with respect—or give her dignity. Don't enter into the consciousness of the pet. That's hard to do, and it would turn this fiction into another genre. 500 words.

ELIZABETH MARSHALL THOMAS writes, at the beginning of her lovely book *The Tribe of Tiger*:

> One summer evening at our home in New Hampshire, my husband and I were startled to see two deer bolt from the woods into our field. No sooner had they cleared the thickets than they stopped, turned around, and, with their white tails high in warning, looked back at something close to the ground as if whatever frightened them also puzzled them. We were wondering aloud what might be threatening the deer when to our astonishment our own cat sprang from the bushes in full charge, ears up, tail high, arms reaching, claws out. The deer fled, and the cat, who fell to earth disappointed, watched them out of sight.

Thomas describes not only her own and her husband's surprise at their cat's fierceness and success as a predator but also their own pride in this seven-pound, two-year-old male cat. Our pets are our children, often before we have children, but even afterwards. They tend to remain the size of infants, so the anomaly of cuddling and baby-talking a sixteen-year-old cat is something we don't have to acknowledge. Our pets are family, and they believe that whatever we want them to do is in their best interests, until they learn bitterly over time that the humans they thought they trusted are not trustworthy.

—————————————————————(**176**)——————————————————————

THE LETTER IN THE DESK. In this exercise, work with a character you're very familiar with—someone from a novel you've abandoned, a series of stories, or at least a story you've worked hard on but have not finished. This character is waiting for someone she knows very well in something like a study or a living room. The wait is long. The event these two people are going to is not pleasant to contemplate—a doctor's office, an IRS audit, or something they both dread. The character gets restless waiting for the friend and begins opening bureau drawers, just browsing through stuff, doing a little light snooping around. The character comes upon a sealed letter, addressed to her. What's in the letter? Why has it been sealed but not delivered? Answer these questions in 500 words.

ALAN ZWEIBEL, A WRITER in the early days of *Saturday Night Live*, said Gilda Radner "used to say that she would search through Lorne [Michaels]'s desk hoping that she'd find a note that said, 'I really like Gilda.'" What does this say of Gilda's relationship to Lorne Michaels, the long-time producer of *Saturday Night Live* and her boss for five years?

They did become very good friends over the years, but Gilda's feelings of inadequacy and her wish to have revealed to her the full extent of Lorne's affection for her are painfully clear from this little imaginary note in his desk. The note is also a touchstone of Gilda Radner's extraordinary sense of humor—vulnerable, insecure, even childlike, and yet strangely assertive and grown-up—the note cuts to the quick of an everyday desire. We all have friends we admire and some friends we need affirmation from. We rarely receive such direct evidence of someone else's love for us. People transmit this information subtly—or the best way to receive this information is indirectly, through action and gesture, rather than straight up. "I love you" means less than a quiet defense of your outstanding skills as a certified public accountant when you're not there to hear this defense of you.

EDUCATION & SCHOOL

We all have experience of schools of various kinds. We've all suffered from the terrors, bullying, anxiety, and relief of (finishing) school. Go back to your old high school and volunteer to do something for the school, as I did sixteen years after I graduated. It was chilling how familiar the halls and classrooms felt (I had not set foot in the building in all that time). I conducted a couple of fiction workshops, and the students were mildly interested, and when I finished I practically ran away from the building, so powerful was its gloom for me still.

— 177 —

COLLEGE. Write a letter home to parents from a student in college who despises college. This student does not hate it because he is doing badly or doesn't have friends. The student dislikes intensely the philosophy of the university or college, disapproves of the assumptions of the faculty,

and most of all profoundly hates his classmates' lighthearted attitude
toward their education. 500 words.

THE POET ROBERT LOWELL wrote this letter to his parents, at the age of nineteen, from Harvard University:

> I consider a *college education* and degree as not only valueless but
> detrimental. One does not meet interesting or useful people. I
> have no interest in college life or athletics of any sort. The cours-
> es (English in particular, also the others) are largely conservative
> hack work conducted by mediocrities. Any profit that I have so far
> gotten, except for a valuable insight into the stupidity of academic
> methods, has been from my own reading etc. almost in spite of
> the authorities.

178

AMONG SCHOOLCHILDREN. Imagine a grade school classroom
(third or fourth grade) with a teacher and twenty students. Another
adult has been observing this classroom for several days or weeks—a
journalist or someone from the upper levels of the school administration. The fiction is from this person's point of view. The teacher has
very little control over the class (and very little confidence in his abilities) but the class has great affection for him. The main point of this
exercise is to study a small group dynamic that has a great deal of
consistency over time. A fourth-grade class meets and stays together
for a whole year. Everyone becomes intimately familiar with everyone
else. 500 words.

———————————— **179** ————————————

THE JEAN COCTEAU REPERTORY. Write a description of several actors trying out for a repertory theater company. A true repertory company puts on four to six plays a year, rotating them around a schedule, so that actors have to play more than one role at a time. Candidates for the acting company may be asked to perform a "psalm from the Bible, a movement mime piece, and a cross-gender Shakespeare passage" (more explained below). Or come up with your own ideas of what sorts of simple, odd performances you would want these actors to do for their tryouts. Don't show us the actual auditions. Give us the conversation that follows. 750 words.

THIS IS FROM a *Playbill* essay on Eve Adamson:

> Eve Adamson founded Jean Cocteau Repertory in 1971. Its first location was on Bond Street off the Bowery—then a dangerous neighborhood unpopulated by theatres. The troupe later moved to its familiar Bowery home inside the landmarked cast-iron French Second Empire building that was once the home of the German Exchange Bank. Here she and her non-Equity ensemble presented a steady diet of classic plays year in and year out. Production values were low, but so were ticket prices, and audiences were attracted by the fine acting of seasoned regulars like Craig Smith, Elise Stone, Harris Berlinsky, Angela Vitale, and Joe Menino.
>
> Her initial vision involved a rotating repertory of time-honored plays performed by a permanent ensemble—an anomaly in New

York theatre, where both the repertory system and permanent acting corps are unusual. The audition process at the Cocteau was arduous. Candidates were asked to perform a psalm from the Bible, a movement mime piece, and a cross-gender Shakespeare passage, among other things. When accepted into the ensemble, they were required to take on parts both large and small, as well as sell tickets, do publicity, and clean out the "moat," a cement gully that surrounded the theatre on two sides and constantly filled up with garbage.

In *Live From New York*, Tom Shales and James Andrew Miller's oral history of *Saturday Night Live*, Bill Murray talks about how John Belushi tried to psych out certain guest hosts of the show:

> The better an actor the host was, the sicker Belushi would be. He would be at death's door, and he was coming in in a robe, unable to speak. He'd have doctors in his dressing room ... The host would be thinking, "Belushi isn't even going to show up, he's too sick even to work"—and then John would come out on the show and just blast them away. He would sucker-punch guys that just didn't see it coming.

The lesson I take from this anecdote is that everything is acting, both onstage and offstage—or that there is nothing offstage to good actor's preparation.

—————————————(**180**)—————————————

PREP SCHOOL. Write about the life of a private school only from the boys' or girls' bathroom in one of the central classroom buildings of the school. Give us two or three short scenes in these utilitarian rooms. Don't go for the expected—boys dunking other boys headfirst into the toilets. Explore the unexpected. If you have no experience with a prep school, don't worry. I am not looking for realism here. I am looking for educated fantasy. 750 words.

WHEN I WAS THIRTEEN, I spent six months at Magdalen College School, a private school in Oxford, England, across a small river from Oxford University's Magdalen College (but apparently unrelated to the more famous namesake). This was 1969, and it seems churlish to complain about a half year spent in England and at a fancy private school, during part of my eighth-grade year (the rest of the year my family traveled across Europe and then we settled down for three months in southern Spain, where my brother, sister, and I did not attend school). Still, this was the worst education experience I ever had.

On the first day, my father met with the headmaster and my brother and me. The headmaster seemed kindly, if a bit absent-minded. He had assigned two boys from our classes to guide us around campus and our classes. The boy he assigned me said, "Right, let's go. First class is starting." I followed him around the corner of a building and ran into him just a few feet away from my father and the headmaster. The boy hissed at me. "Listen, Yank, if you think I'm going to show you around school, you're mistaken. Bugger off."

I had no idea what this phrase meant, but it sounded unfriendly. I considered turning around and asking the headmaster for another guide. That seemed unthinkable, so I chose to follow the boy at a safe distance, assuming he was going to my first class, too. This was the beginning of many such adventures. My brother, a year older, did not seem to have nearly as much trouble as I did, although he also felt the place was pretty unfriendly.

—————————————————— **181** ——————————————————

DAYDREAMS. Observe both the reality of an eighth-grade classroom situation around one particular student, and this student's daydreams. Indicate the reality with regular font and the daydreams with *italics*. Separate the two realities by paragraph breaks. Make this a class you took—French, Algebra, Social Studies. Honor the subject and do a little research into it to try to make the teacher's presentation realistic and not completely ridiculous, although you can play with this a bit. The idea is to follow a wandering mind, infected occasionally by the subject being taught, caught off-guard constantly by the small pleasures and great horrors of the thirteen-year-old psyche. Don't make these daydreams rank fantasies, but rather try to keep the daydreams as plausible as the classroom reality is. 750 words.

—————————————————— **182** ——————————————————

BOYS & GIRLS. Write about a war between boys and girls in a fifth-grade class. Not all of the boys and girls of the class participate in the war, but all have to take sides at least tacitly. Fifth grade is at the front end of puberty and hormonal changes. Girls are physically more advanced and bigger at that age. Boys are boys—a different breed. This can be a subtle or overt battle of the sexes. It may end up an allegory for what happens at that period in children's lives, not necessarily a realistic drama. 750 words.

ADRIAN FURNHAM, interviewed in *Newsweek*, spoke of differences in men and women. He is a professor of psychology at University College London, and he notes that men and women have roughly the same I.Q. levels. Furnham says,

> Men aren't more clever or smarter. But since they think they are, they are more confident about their abilities. These self-beliefs, however, may be highly adaptive. Who gets a job? A bright woman who doesn't think she's smart, or a not-so-bright man who believes he's capable of anything? Arrogance and hubris are not attractive qualities, but confident, self-belief may be. Certainly, underestimating abilities might hurt you. There's a good quote from ... Henry Ford. He says: "Whether you believe you can do a thing or not, you are right." And that is what is troublesome. Beliefs may be more important than actual ability in certain settings.

U.S. colleges skew applications so more boys will get in to college than otherwise would (if there were no such affirmative action for high school boys, the percentage of females in college would be over 60 percent, instead of what it is now, 55 percent).

183

MIRRORING. Write a fragment of a scene in later grade school that describes mirroring behavior. Children imitate each other or parents and follow the herd. Try to capture one child echoing and mimicking another child—consciously and unconsciously. The child being mirrored and the child doing the mirroring are not related. 500 words.

RICHARD CONNIFF, in the *New York Times*, notes that humans have a "tendency to synchronize movements":

> One person at the table reaches for his drink and a moment later everyone else also takes a sip. One person in the room stands and stretches, and his neighbors do the same. Walking together, we match strides so closely that armies traditionally learned to break step when crossing a bridge, lest they make it vibrate to the point of collapse ... Mirroring facial expressions can be a survival mechanism. Let's say you're standing around listening to a co-worker gripe about your boss, Thimblebrain. You happen to look up and spot Thimblebrain bearing down on you. It takes just two hundred milliseconds, a fifth of a second, for a look of alarm to flash across your face. The identical expression leaps from your face to the faces of the people around you, causing them to feel fear, too. The conversation dies away just in time. And all this happens before anybody can say, "It's him."
>
> Studies suggest that we like a conversational partner more if the other person has subtly mimicked us. Mirroring gestures and movements also seems to help people work better together. They find a shared rhythm and gradually coalesce into a team, so the parts of a project get handed on seamlessly, as if by magic. One person starts a sentence and the other person finishes it. One comes up with a new product idea and the other nudges it in a new direction.

PLACE

Setting is the period in time or the place in which the events of a story occur. This was one of the options we had when we wrote about novels in my high school English classes. I often chose this option because it seemed easy, but when I got down to it I did not know much about Yoknapatawpha County in Mississippi or Wessex County in England (both fictional places), and I had no idea how to research them. I usually ended up yammering on about the natural world in these novels.

What makes the location of a story vivid is what makes it human. Faulkner's Mississippi is humid, subtropical, and dark green with red dirt, but its scars of slavery and a lost war cannot be described yet can't be avoided. The town I grew up in was a dying mill town that had a college for women in its midst. When I left for college in 1974, the *The Insiders' Guide to the Colleges* complained that Northampton closed shop at six in the evening, and all that stayed open after that was the Dunkin' Donuts. By 1984, that was a laughable statement. When the drinking age was briefly lowered to eighteen in the early 1970s, the town began to flourish as a magnet for young people who were no longer in college (bars began to cater to Smith College students, as well as these newcomers). Now Northampton is cool, an epicenter of food, music, and the arts, with a substantial lesbian population.

Get to know your hometown—or your hometowns. Do research. Go out and interview people—friends, family, and the person who was mayor ten years ago. You write best about the places you know best, but you may not know your own locales as well as you think.

— 184 ⟩————————————

MYTHOLOGIZING HOME. Write a short fragment of prose—which is not fiction—in which you venerate your own home state. Do some research first. Find out the state bird, the state lizard, the biggest cash crop, the last politician to commit suicide while in office. Write as if for an official report, in advertising or chamber of commerce language. Include your own life story around the edges of this fake pamphlet. 750 words.

MICHAEL MARTONE has been mythologizing his home state, Indiana, for many years now. His books include *Fort Wayne Is Seventh on Hitler's List, Alive and Dead in Indiana, Pensées: The Thoughts of Dan Quayle,* and *The Flatness and Other Landscapes,* among many other wonderful books. You get the picture of his approach, maybe, from the titles alone.

— 185 ⟩————————————

BIGGAR. Imagine this small town without doing any research (though I'll give you some small dollop of detail below). Biggar, Saskatchewan, is whatever you want to make of it, except for the sign outside of town on the highways leading into Biggar. Write a fragment of fiction about this place. Populate it with whomever you'd like. Most of these people will be Canadians, but other than that you're free to do whatever you wish. This is an exercise to challenge you to take a real place and fictionalize it, based on nothing more than your own sense of what it might be like and what you want it to be. This is also an exercise in imagining your way into the life of a very small town. If you're a city person, or someone who grew up in a town of even thirty thousand (as I did), you may have difficulty imagining the world of a village with 432 souls (for example—I'm not saying Biggar is that big or small). 750 words.

MY GRANDFATHER TOLD me a story of Biggar, which, he said, once faced a serious moral dilemma. *Reader's Digest* reported, in one of its tiny, stand-alone sections, that there was a road sign outside of Biggar: "New York may be big, but this is Biggar." The trouble was there was no such sign. The townspeople got together and agreed that it was wrong that *Reader's Digest* was reporting a falsehood, so they raised a little money and erected a sign outside of town that said, "New York may be big, but this is Biggar." As nice as this story is, it doesn't seem to be true. I looked up Biggar in Google, and the sign is certainly there, but according to the town fathers (or the webmaster), the sign has been there since the 1920s, and there is no mention of *Reader's Digest*.

Reader's Digest was founded in the 1920s. In 1950, it was far and away the magazine with the largest circulation in the United States. It still has a circulation of more than ten million readers, and perhaps more than thirty million total readers each week (because it lies around in doctors' offices and church foyers). It works on the simple idea of retelling stories from other magazines, in condensed form. *Reader's Digest* novels operate on the same model—turning a five-hundred-page novel into two hundred pages. I don't know if they still publish these condensed novels. *Reader's Digest* is known for telling the truth, but that is not always the case, as we observe here.

──────────────(**186**)──────────────

THE UNITED STATES & CANADA. Write a fragment of fiction about high school sweethearts who live in two towns very close to each other but separated by the U.S.–Canada border, say Oroville, Washington, and Osoyoos, British Columbia, both of which are on Osoyoos Lake; or Vanceboro, Maine, and St. Croix, New Brunswick. They might be children of prominent citizens of these very small towns. They watch the same TV shows, listen to the same radio stations, read the same newspapers (sometimes), and they've grown up in very similar surroundings. But one is Canadian and one is American. Explore the differences between these two cultures. Do some research. 500 words.

WHAT ARE THE DIFFERENCES between these two countries? My father grew up in Calgary, Alberta, and he moved to the United States for his first year of college, and I have many relatives across the border. One of the simple differences is size. In population, the United States vastly outnumbers Canada. In geographical area, Canada is larger, although much of that land is inhabited only by mosquitoes and reindeer. Over 90 percent of the population of Canada lives within one hundred miles of the United States, which clearly is because of the more temperate climate close to the border, not because of love of the United States.

These are two subtly different types of democracies. J. Bartlet Brebner, in *Canada: A Modern History*, says,

> Perhaps the most striking thing about Canada is that it is not the United States. Somehow more than half of North America has

escaped being engulfed by its imminently more powerful neighbor although that neighbor has expanded fairly continuously in North America and elsewhere ...

187

A U.S. TOWN. Present both the relatively modern version (though it may be slightly historical, like 1952 Biloxi or 1985 Oshkosh) and a version of the same place one hundred years before. Write about one historical moment for two paragraphs; then about the other modern moment for two paragraphs. For the last sentences of the piece, alternate sentence by sentence between modern and older town, making sure the reader can reasonably understand this alternation. This exercise should be seven paragraphs and about 750 words long.

188

LOST. Write about a town that has disappeared. It could be a Palestinian village on a hillside in what is now Israel, forcibly evacuated in 1948 and then "erased" from maps and view (though there are vegetable remains of the town that show its outlines from the air). It could be a ghost town in the American West—a silver or gold rush boomtown that remains in substantial form but is empty of people. It could be an African town erased by the encroaching Sahara. There are also new ghost towns on the Great Plains in Kansas, Nebraska, and the Dakotas, which are slowly (or sometimes quickly) depopulating. Or it could be a village sunk under the Quabbin Reservoir, which was made in 1933 in Massachusetts.

Write about it at three different times: in the present; at the moment of its last human habitation; and at its most vibrant, lively apex. In other words, write the history of this town backwards. 500 words.

— 189 —

BIOGRAPHY OF A COUNTRY. Write a biography of a real country. This will have to be ridiculously condensed. Or you may choose three or four exemplary tiny stories to stand for this country. 250 words.

METONYMY IS A CRUCIAL term of art for travel writing (an example of metonymy is *the crown* standing for the queen). We see something and we're desperate to make it mean something else or mean some much larger thing. We create narrative where it does not exist, because we're narrative-minded. We create metonymy in the same way. Travelers often see the worlds they visit in ways no local could possibly see them—travelers have the keys to the local myths, but they can't communicate these myths to the locals. That's your job here. Find a handful of metonymic images or symbols that stand for a whole country.

— 190 —

NAKED CITY. "There are eight million stories in the Naked City. This has been one of them." Those were the closing lines of the voice-over narration of the TV show *Naked City*, which ran from 1959 to 1963. For this exercise, write an examination of a big city—Chicago, Los Angeles, Mexico City, Tokyo, Cairo, New York, or any place you know well. This study will be something like the Biography of a Country exercise (189), except you will have a little more room to populate the city with brief brushstroke portraits of its inhabitants. 500 words.

NAKED CITY WAS a police drama that broke new ground for TV dramas—no neat resolutions and trials for every episode, like *Dragnet*, which was on the air around the same time. The show also introduced the novelty of location shoots, many in the south Bronx near where the series was produced, and New York City became its biggest star. The series was inspired by a 1948 film of the same name by Jules Dassin, one of the prototypical film noirs of that period.

FOOD & DRINK

Food is a basic necessity and one of the great pleasures of our lives. A beautifully prepared meal can rest in our memory more securely than our first sexual encounter. M.F.K. Fisher, the author of *How to Cook a Wolf* and *The Gastronomical Me*, among many other great books about food, says it best:

> People ask me: Why do you write about food, and eating and drinking? Why don't you write about the struggle for power and security, and about love, the way others do? They ask it accusingly, as if I were somehow gross, unfaithful to the honor of my craft. The easiest answer is to say that, like most humans, I am hungry. But there is more than that. It seems to me that our three basic needs, for food and security and love, are so mixed and mingled and entwined that we cannot straightly think of one without the others. So it happens

that when I write of hunger, I am really writing about love and the hunger for it, and warmth and the love of it and the hunger for it.

─────────────── **191** ───────────────

ABALONE. Write about a meal at the center of which is an unusual food like abalone. If you've had experience with truffles, escargot, eel, or any rarely served foods, use your own sense memory as guide. But you can also do research into the food. We resist food we're not familiar with—food that looks odd or even disturbing. The first people to eat lobster were either very daring or very hungry. Tomatoes were considered poisonous until the late eighteenth century (they are part of the deadly nightshade family and their leaves are toxic).

In this exercise, don't try to make your readers squeamish. Explore the pleasures a rare taste can give people. 750 words.

RUTH REICHL (in *American Food Writing: An Anthology With Classic Recipes*, edited by Molly O'Neill) describes beautifully the evocations of other tastes this one mollusk triggers:

> The abalone was ... more like some exotic mushroom than something from the ocean, with a slightly musky flavor that made me think of ferns. Beside it the geoduck was pure ocean—crisp and briny and in-credibly clean ... Next to the pure austerity of these two, the Japanese clam seemed lush and almost baroque in its sensuality.

Notice how Reichl reaches for both other food tastes and plants we don't eat (ferns) to create in our minds the experience of eating this food. My wife and I had escargot in France on a barge trip along the River Marne, although the chef would not disclose the mystery at the center of the meal.

I was delighted—by the sauce as much as by the flavor of these snails. Cynthia wouldn't be snookered into the trick. She guessed what the mystery meat was and whispered it to our Cockney waitress, who giggled and said she wouldn't eat the food either—"they taste like worms." They did indeed taste of earth, but that's something I like in other foods, like broccoli rabe or venison, so I was happy.

192

ALCOHOL. Write a short exercise about a person who is drunk but forced by circumstances to observe a complex situation and improvise a set of solutions to the situation. The person who has had too much to drink may be a chronic drunk—an alcoholic—or an occasional drinker who has had too much to drink. Don't worry too much about this background; just lay it out plainly for us. The problem of this exercise will be to watch a character struggle to master his disorientation. Alcohol interferes with many of our senses. Our vision can be blurred. Our thoughts scatter and divide and don't stay focused. We become more emotionally direct and open, though we also try to hide our drunkenness. 750 words.

AS THE INESTIMABLE Homer Simpson says, alcohol is "the cause of, and solution to, all our problems." In the first five years I taught fiction writing, from 1993 to 1998 or so, I would implore my undergraduates not to write about heavy drinking in their fiction, in part because it was a common, romantic subject. I warned them that the state of inebriation was very difficult to portray. It demanded much more of them as writers than they realized. It was also generally boring to read about. Someone else's night of excess drinking is not enjoyable to witness. It's not even all that fun if you're experiencing it yourself.

193

BACON IN EGYPT. Think of the experience of missing a food from home when you are traveling for a long while. What happens when you actually eat this food? This exercise is about food and about homesickness. Put that at the center of your fragment of a narrative. Travel is about leaving behind the world you know and experiencing, if only temporarily, the sense of exile, even though you know you will return. Travelers almost always return. 500 words.

BOTH MUSLIMS AND JEWS refrain from eating pork. Coptic Christians (the ancient Egyptian sect of Christians) revel in such foods and drink that antagonize their Muslim brethren. The Copts make up about 12 percent of the population of Egypt. When I lived in Cairo in the late 1980s, my neighbors down the hall had me over for meals regularly. I was the lonely bachelor down the hall, and I babysat occasionally for their two young children in an unequal exchange. A few months after arriving there, I noticed a smell emanating from Allen and Nora's apartment (we had adjoining flats). I think I floated down the hall on the scent of frying bacon, a very rare aroma during this time I'd been away from the United States. At home I'd never been much of a fan of bacon. In Egypt, I was overwhelmed by the desire for this illicit, rare food.

My family drove through Europe in 1969 and 1970. The first leg of the trip was by car from Sweden into Russia and eventually down to Spain. That initial month of travel was behind the Iron Curtain, and the food rarely met with we three children's approval. When we arrived in Vienna, outside Communist Europe, we drove past a Wimpy hamburger restaurant. It was not a familiar chain to us (we were used to McDonald's and Kentucky Fried Chicken), but we kids demanded our father stop at the restaurant. We ordered Wimpy Burgers, and we were crushed to discover they were more like sausages in buns. As a kid I had not been opposed to sausage, but I'd been expecting a hamburger experience and I did not get one.

─────────────── 194)───────────────

LOBSTER BISQUE. Write several small fragments of scenes about a wonderful, memorable meal prepared by amateurs (not a meal in a restaurant). Use fragments of recipes, too. Allow the human characters in the piece to recede a bit—give us no names for the diners. Only the food and its preparation should have names. Each fragment should be no more than 200 words. The total piece should be no more than 750 words.

IN 1990, IN PROVINCETOWN, Massachusetts, my wife Cynthia and I, my parents, my sister and her husband Pete, and my brother all gathered for a few days in July. We were all staying at different places. My brother was living in P'town for the summer. Cynthia and I were borrowing a friend's apartment. My parents and my sister and her husband were visiting for a week. My brother, who had been a cook at a SoHo Italian restaurant in New York until recently, decided to make a lavish dinner for us.

One aspect of the dinner was the lobster bisque, which took several days to prepare. He brought the lobsters home alive, as one does. I was there for this first part of the preparation. I was expecting the usual method of dropping the crustaceans into boiling water. But my brother took out a huge meat cleaver, placed each lobster on a cutting board, and, with a swift and sure swing, cut the lobsters in half, lengthwise down the body. Then he put the lobsters in several pots and added onions and various other stock ingredients, and let these pots simmer for two days until the lobster stock was ready. This simple fact of multiple-day preparation changed everyone's attitude toward this dinner. We'd arrive at Geoff's apartment, smell this stock in the making, and become subtly more excited each time we savored the process. The meal itself wasn't a letdown—we also had steak *au poivre* and probably another few things as well. The lobster bisque itself was just the appetizer. It had cream, butter, garlic, and this magnificent stock. We all ate it and were ravished by the taste. We were also full after just one small bowl of the soup, and the rest of the dinner was difficult to finish. Nevertheless, we all speak of that meal with just the words, *lobster bisque*, and we're brought back to an extraordinary memory.

Read Harry Mathews's story "Country Cooking From Central France: Roast Boned Rolled Stuffed Shoulder of Lamb," from his collection *The Human Country*. The meal described in the story (it reads like a long recipe that breaks down into narrative) is nearly impossible to imagine, let alone make—meat stuffed inside fowl stuffed inside different fowl of various kinds.

MONEY & CLASS

Max Rodenbeck, in *Cairo: The City Victorious*, talks about extreme poverty in Egypt:

> The inhabitants of Imbaba seldom look on their neighborhoods as slums. Sewage may be leaky or nonexistent, electricity sporadic, but the Popular Quarters boast a congenial intimacy that is rarely tainted badly by urban blights such as crime and juvenile delinquency. Considering the depth of poverty in some parts of the city, the overall level of public safety is remarkable. Perhaps this is because, despite Cairo's size, most of its people still live in village-scale compartments. They know their neighbors. They care for their family reputations. They look on their small world as real.

There are many different kinds of poverty in the world, just as there are many kinds of wealth. Rodenbeck describes what one might also call the happy poor. I lived just across the Nile from this neighborhood, from 1987 to 1989, and I can corroborate that there seemed to be a festive atmosphere in Imbaba most of the time, whereas on the rich secluded island I lived on, Zamalek, there was a gloomy and slightly eerie quiet. In these exercises I hope to inspire you to write about wealth, class, poverty, and inequality, which may not be subjects you're used to tackling in your fiction.

─────────────────────── **195** ───────────────────────

SWEARING. Write a short piece of narrative in which there are two classes of characters. One class is rich, articulate, well educated (though this does not mean they are smart). The other group is poor, speaks in an underclass dialect of the same language, and keeps their resentment for the rich carefully under wraps. The working class representatives in your little democracy also swear a great deal, or some of them do. Figure out a situation in which both groups are distressed enough to reveal their usually hidden prejudices. The situation also should cause the working class group to let loose with their favorite adjectives. Don't be shy, but don't go overboard. 750 words.

IN ENGLISH, SWEAR WORDS were the older Anglo-Saxon words, after the Normans conquered England and brought French with them (in 1066). Just as there needed to be two words to describe a crime when arresting a suspected felon (assault and battery, the one French and the other English), there developed two layers of words for activities the upper classes didn't want to speak of. To *fuck* someone, or to say it out loud, was wrong. One *fornicated*. It was also permissible to say *defecation*, but not *shit*. Swear words like these were relegated to taboo because of class notions. The lower classes swore; the ruling class spoke in a refined language even when they were saying naughty things.

─────────────────────── **196** ───────────────────────

THE CORPORATION VS. THE INDIVIDUAL. Construct a fragment of a battle between a corporation and an individual. The corporation will be represented by individual human beings, but let these people speak with the authority and carelessness of that inhuman entity, the corporation. The battle does not have to be large. It also does not have to be in person. Much of what goes on between individuals and corporations is carried on over the phone, by e-mail, and by mail. A corporation is not an individual but has all the rights of one. 500 words.

197

MONEY. In one short scene, show us a character that has relatively little money—say $503 in her checking account and $3,006 in credit card debt. In the next scene, show us this same character suddenly very wealthy. Don't worry too much about how the character got this money—an inheritance, a lottery winning, or an unforeseen windfall from an anonymous benefactor. What is the difference between these two states of being? How has the character changed? Mark Twain noted that "unexpected money is a delight. The same sum is a bitterness when you expected more." But Mark Twain also said, "It is better to take what does not belong to you than to let it lie around neglected." 500 words.

198

CLASS DISMISSED. Write a political response to what Princess Diana's grandfather is reputed to have said, that he "didn't see the point of ordinary people." Imagine the moments surrounding someone saying something like this. Use this phrase in your exercise. How could a whole useless class of people like this family and the British aristocracy operate and keep their moral bearings? You may feel that Diana herself was somehow above (or below) this family of hers, that she fought her way to some kind of nobility and purpose in life. I don't believe that, but put aside whatever feelings you have for the People's Princess. Write a scathing indictment of this class of people, part essay, part fiction. 500 words.

IT IS TINA BROWN, in her book *The Diana Chronicles*, who claims that Princess Diana's grandfather said he "didn't see the point of ordinary people." Do we have such a class (as the Spencers) in the United States? Who are the Bushes? What is Paris Hilton? Our royalty has tended to be of the Hollywood variety, built out of talent, at least at some point in the royal's career (leaving Bush and Paris Hilton out of this argument). Janet Maslin, reviewing *The Diana Chronicles* for *The New York Times*, says, "Like any writer examining the life and death of Diana, Princess of Wales, Tina Brown must peer into the world of British royalty with nose pressed to the glass. Unlike almost all of the others, Ms. Brown does not fog the windowpanes." Even this review's careful distancing of itself from the notion that royalty and the upper classes are somehow better than the rest of us does not prevent it from gushing about this feat of Tina Brown's (it is a nice turn of phrase). The actual implication of the fact that Ms. Brown does not fog the windowpanes as she's peeping in on the lives of the royal family is that she must not be alive herself—she has no breath with which to fog windows—or that she too is a kind of royal. F. Scott Fitzgerald told his friend Hemingway, "The rich are different than you and me." Fitzgerald was famously obsessed with money and the super rich. Hemingway replied, just as famously, "Yes, they have more money."

───────────────── 199 ─────────────────

THE CAMP. Write a short incomplete piece of narrative about a remote playground for a family with old money somewhere in North America. Imagine a handful of people with a great deal of money and privilege, in a hunting lodge or large mansion in the woods or on a lake. They are trapped in this place, unable to communicate with the outside world, prisoners in a lavishly well-supplied jail. Will these be wonderful, well-adjusted, kind people? Are the rich automatically happier or smarter than the middle classes? Be hard on these characters, but be fair. 750 words.

HERE IS LUC SANTE's stylish beginning of his *New York Times* review of Russell Banks's book *The Reserve*:

> It is 1936, and we are in the Adirondacks, at a party at a luxurious camp on a vast private reserve. ("Camp" is a local upper-caste understatement, comparable to the use of "cottage" in Newport, R.I.) As the sun begins to dip behind the mountain range that dominates the horizon, a beautiful young woman detaches herself from her elders and walks barefoot to the shore of the lake. Suddenly a seaplane appears in the air and all look on, stunned, as it lands on the surface of the water. Such a thing has never before occurred, and furthermore is taboo under the largely unspoken laws of the reserve. A dashing aviator—we will discover that he is a famous artist, a radical, a free spirit—steps out of the plane and locks eyes with the glamorous yet troubled young woman.

—————————————————(**200**)—————————————————

MARLON BRANDO. Quincy Jones, an old friend of Marlon Brando's from the early 1950s, said Brando's refrain in those days, when he wanted to go out at night and have fun, was "Let's go out and jiggle some molecules." Another friend said you lined up like iron filings toward Marlon Brando's talent. What these people are describing is Brando's electrifying personality—as an actor and as a celebrity. He was the most influential actor of his generation. Even Elvis Presley admitted he was imitating Brando, from the movie *The Wild One*, early in his own singing career. As an adult Brando was wealthy and of the far reaches of the upper classes by means of his acting abilities, though he was born solidly in the middle class. Try to imagine another person like this, world-famous because of talent and hard work, who could make iron filings line up toward his talent. Describe this person without presenting him to us directly. Let us overhear a few of his friends or sycophants, hanging around talking about this person, waiting for him to arrive. 500 words.

THE
APPENDICES

MY REFERENCE BOOKS

These are my reference books in the order they sit on my shelves, just to the right of my desk. One of my undergraduate students asked me for this list a few years ago. I've slowly assembled these books over the years as ready-at-hand research for writing fiction and nonfiction, and for my teaching. I also use Google, *Wikipedia*, and the *Oxford English Dictionary* online (which I have access to through my university library), but I love these solid, useful, surprising books.

A People's History of the United States, Howard Zinn

The Columbia History of the 20th Century, Richard W. Bulliet (editor)

The New Penguin History of the World, J.M. Roberts

Atlantic Brief Lives, Louis Kronenberger (editor)

Mrs. Byrne's Dictionary of Unusual, Obscure, and Preposterous Words, Josepha H. Byrne

100 Ways of Seeing an Unequal World, Bob Sutcliffe

The Penguin Dictionary of Epigrams, Mark Cohen

Dictionary of Philosophy and Religion, William L. Reese

The New York Public Library American History Desk Reference, Douglas Brinkley

Encyclopedia of American History, Richard B. Morris

One Hundred Twentieth-Century Philosophers, Stuart Brown, Diané Collinson, Robert Wilkinson

Brief Lives, John Aubrey

French Dictionary

Egyptian Arabic Phrasebook, Siona Jenkins

The Primary Colors, Alexander Theroux

Roget's Thesaurus

The Book of the Mind, Stephen Wilson

The Subjective Self, Harwood Fisher

A Glossary of Literary Terms, M.H. Abrams

The Penguin Dictionary of Critical Theory, David Macey

Critical Theory Since 1965, Hazard Adams and Leroy Searle

The Macmillan Visual Dictionary (a backwards dictionary— visual details are named)

New England Indians, C. Keith Wilbur

Secondary School Atlas

The Anchor Atlas of World History, Hermann Kinder

Weather, Armand Spitz

A Field Guide to Trees and Shrubs, George A. Petrides

Brewer's Dictionary of Phrase & Fable

The Oxford Companion to the English Language

Webster's Dictionary of English Usage

The Treasury of the Encyclopedia Britannica, Clifton Fadiman (editor)

An Introduction to the Languages of the World, Anatole Lyovin

The New Biographical Dictionary of Film, David Thomson

The Holy Bible

The Oxford Universal Dictionary

Merriam-Webster's Collegiate Dictionary

The Official SCRABBLE Players Dictionary

The Columbia History of Western Philosophy, Richard H. Popkin (editor)

ADVICE FOR TEACHERS AND STUDENTS

A system with interchangeable parts. My fiction workshops are spare parts warehouses young writers enter to ransack (and create) fragments that can be fitted together to build a story (or many stories). Exercises can be more than convenient tools for triggering conversation about fiction before the group gets down to the real work of discussing longer stories.

Exercises are the heart of the process of teaching fiction in my workshops. Students select exercises from my own collection of fiction exercises. They also design their own exercises and algorithms (procedures for solving a creative problem). Students do two sets of five exercises in the first few weeks of the term, with a consistent set of characters, place, and time, but I urge them *not* to write a story. We read these exercises, and the *class* looks for a story or several stories. We often suggest two or three or parts of several exercises as the building blocks for the longer story they will write and give to us for the third workshop of their work. In other words, the class and I are on the lookout for an unusual combination of fragments to make another story than the writer may have had in mind. The effect of this collage is to show the whole class the many possibilities of narrative.

I want the class to see fiction as a system with interchangeable working parts. A side benefit of talking about small pieces of prose (the exercises are usually less than two pages) is that we can talk about language, paragraphs, and sentences, which is harder to do when you're struggling to describe how a fifteen-page story works. Most fiction workshops seem resigned to the idea that young writers ought not to be interfered with while they're dreaming up their stories. But creativity can be taught.

Before writing. Poets have used exercises for thousands of years—and in poetry workshops from the beginning. Fiction exercises are also fairly common, although the main use of them has been as prompts, to get students moving toward a short story, or as ways to discuss components of fiction.

I am very interested in the composition of fiction and a little less interested in the revision of fiction, which has been the most common emphasis of fiction workshops. The standard workshop says, "Bring in a story and we'll help you revise it." That did not satisfy me. Revision is a well-traveled road in the discussion of fiction. We know how it's done. Few writers do it as well as they'd like to, but it is a matter of looking hard at the rough drafts of your work and having the courage and clarity to reorganize large chunks of the manuscript and throw out beautiful writing that doesn't help the whole piece.

In the matter of beginnings, there are not as many paths through the wilderness. The Oulipo writers have experimented fruitfully with the basic idea of how to enliven the work before pen touches paper, how to make the process fun and experimental in the true sense of the word. The French word for experiment is *experience*, which means both experiment and experience when translated. Experience is an experiment. An old meaning of the English word *experiment* was also experience, but it now means test or trial, a *tentative* procedure or policy. Oulipo has made experiments in fiction fun and ends in themselves. No one quarrels with the idea of scientific experiment. Why question the value of trial and error in fiction?

Data beautification. In the journal *Nature*, the editors spoke of a problem of academic scientists rushing to publish their work before it is ready. They note that some

> ... scientists do not take the time to understand complex data-acquisition tools and occasionally seem to be duped by the ease of use of image-processing programs to manipulate data in a manner that amounts to misrepresentation. The intention is usually not to deceive but to make the story more striking by presenting clear-cut, selected, or simplified data—an approach we have dubbed "data beautification."

This in a nutshell is what's wrong with the typical creative writing workshop. Teachers seek to simplify and beautify the component parts of their students' fiction. Avoid this. Allow your fiction to be irregular and jagged. Symmetry is certainly a worthwhile goal in art (as it is in nature), but it should not be the only goal. Let this book guide you toward unusual shapes and orders that look disorderly. Be comfortable with a bit of chaos.

The trouble with seeking symmetry and beauty before you're done with a project is that you rob yourself of useful and inventive solutions to the story or novel. Creativity thrives on chaos and confusion, not on clarity and simplicity.

The tradition. The workshop should also situate the student writer in a tradition of other writings. I often have two dueling texts, to show very different approaches to fiction and the craft of fiction. But I think more and more that workshops and literary history courses should resemble each other. There need be no wall between the two types of classes.

Literary studies classes wisely avoid examining the idea of authors' intentions (although perhaps they go too far in this prohibition). We can't know what an author was thinking when she wrote a poem or a novel, even with a very elaborately annotated manuscript, but that doesn't mean there isn't evidence of the construction of the poem or novel quite visible in its structure and expression. The type of literary criticism called New Historicism worries about the long stream of interrelated events, social forces, and texts that makes up history. The idea that there is an author flies in the face of a lot of theoretical and philosophical thinking that underpins much literary study. But literature is an important force all by itself, a way of looking at the world, and a reflection of human consciousness, which might be just as important as the historical events surrounding literature.

Donald Barthelme's questions. I was a graduate student in the last fiction workshop Donald Barthelme taught at The City College of New York in the spring of 1983. Just after that he began teaching full time at the University of Houston. In most fiction workshops, students hand out copies of stories in advance of the next class, and both the students and the teacher have plenty of time to read through them. Barthelme required that we all experience the stories together, without even having a photocopy of the story in class. Some would violate this rule and read copies surreptitiously circulated, samizdat fashion. He argued that we needed to learn how to hear stories and respond to them only that way. So the student would read the story, and Barthelme would ask tough questions of the rest of us (never the writer). If a question was not answered to Don's satisfaction, he asked a different question of another student, leaving no time to think of interesting and entertaining answers to the last question.

Gallows humor. For instance, if someone else had read aloud Barthelme's own story "Some of Us Had Been Threatening Our Friend Colby" (a light tale of some friends who decide a friend has gone "too far" and should be hanged), Don might then have told us the story of a condemned man in Greece forced to walk across a wide valley to the only tree large enough to hang him. After walking for a while, the condemned man says to the priest and the constable that being made to walk all this way in this heat is cruel and unusual punishment. The priest says, "Well, at least you don't have to walk back to the village." Then Don might have asked, "How does this writer find humor in a hanging?" Barthelme's questions mirrored the incredible efficiency in his own writing. He tried to train us to cut to the quick, to find the heart of the problem in our fiction. I loved this stern Socratic method, Don moving things along without the usual blather of a workshop. Nor did he need to hear from everyone about each story.

When he'd heard enough interesting things he'd be satisfied. So we learned how to listen to fiction, as much as how to read it, and exercised different muscles than we were all used to.

Fathers & sons. I read three pages of what turned out to be my first novel, *Still Life With Insects*, in one class. Barthelme seemed interested in the story, and he invited me to meet with him several times over the summer to work on it. He asked what time I'd like to meet, noting casually that he allowed himself to drink Scotch after five. Let's meet at five, I said. One day he described a dream he'd had the night before. He was in a room filled with hardbound and paperback versions of his books. His father, the modernist architect, was also in the room, absent-mindedly examining one of these books. Finally, after a long silence, he walked over to his son and hit him on the forehead with the book. "Why don't you get a real job, Don?" It was reassuring, if a bit chilling, to know that a renowned writer could have the same sort of dreams I was having. After nearly every class that semester, the group would invite Don to join us for a drink. He arrived only once, at the Cedar Tavern, where he and the abstract expressionists had often met in the early sixties. He wore a cowboy hat, along with his usual cowboy boots. He was shy in this setting, chatting quietly with one or two students, no longer our teacher, just an eccentric-looking Texan out of place in New York City.

A reader's paradise. Donald Barthelme instilled in me the desire to understand the world literately and literally, as a reader and thinker. Most writers are diffident about being in the academy. Don showed us that we could explore the process of making our art intellectually, intelligently, and efficiently. He also used these questions to instruct his students to be better readers—reading seemed as important as writing. Don's fiction has always been a reader's paradise, a field littered with fragments of advertising, philosophy, art, and other fiction. If you look closely, you'll see his writing is filled with questions, too, a simple method of turning the story on a dime, changing the rhythm or speed. They are questions the reader might have asked himself if he'd thought of them.

A CONVERSATION ABOUT TEACHING
FICTION EXERCISES

Janet Bland and I had this dialogue with each other about teaching fiction exercises a year ago. Janet teaches at Marietta College in Ohio. She is the author of *A Fish Full of River* and co-author of *The Civil Mind*. Janet was a graduate student of mine, and she also directed the First-Year Composition program at the University of Denver for a year before moving on to Ohio. She has probably taught *The 3 A.M. Epiphany* more than anyone else, other than me.

Janet Bland: What do you say to the students, particularly graduate students, who don't want to do exercises? What might you say to get around the resistance?

Brian Kiteley: I say, relax. Most of my graduate students resist the notion that they ought to do exercises. At DU, they are Ph.D. students who have already taken half a dozen workshops. I understand their resistance, but I do what I can to melt it. I am a pretty sophisticated writer, with thirty years of writing experience, and I use exercises all the time. I like the feeling of being told to look this one direction (toward a sunrise, for instance) and discover that the fragment of a story I need is crawling toward me from the darkness behind me. All writing is based on some kind of resistance or restraint. Writers just don't know what the restraints are most of the time. It pays to learn how to use restraint and discipline.

Janet Bland: How might the use of exercises shape the nature or trajectory of a fiction workshop?

Brian Kiteley: Your method of teaching these exercises, Janet, sounds like a way to use exercises (or groups of them as I've organized the exercises in *The 3 A.M. Epiphany*) to shape the trajectory of a workshop. As I understand your approach, you have the class do a set of exercises on conversation or dialogue, and then you discuss a handful of the exercises the students bring in. All discussion circles around the experience of writing about two or three people talking, rather than the disembodied process of dialogue in a Denis Johnson story, for instance (as good as Johnson is, students rarely inhabit a story they've read for class the way they inhabit something they've written). I don't deny the value of reading great fiction for workshops, but there is also something very much more effective about teaching by doing.

Janet Bland: You know, Brian, as much as young writers, undergrad or grad student, allow themselves to be overwhelmed at times by the abilities of their favorite writers, allow themselves to be stuck in the obvious contrast between their work and the work of those they admire, I believe that what they want most is to discover their own literary selves. I believe that no matter how daunting the task, students want to find their own sound. I think using exercises helps them break down fiction writing into its essential elements. Sure it's fun to read dialogue written by a greatly admired writer, but that's not really the purpose of the workshop. I tell my students that these exercises are like strength training—we isolate the creative muscle groups (character, setting, point of view) and work them until they are strong.

Brian Kiteley: So how did you overcome your resistance to my exercises, Janet? What did you discover when you did some of the exercises?

Janet Bland: I did not want to write the exercises. I remember quite clearly thinking that I was being underestimated, that an exercise was akin to training wheels and I was so beyond that sort of thing. I was writing whole stories, after all. But once I resigned myself to the task at hand, I was surprised by what I was able to accomplish within the focus of the exercise. I was asked to begin a story (maybe one page long?) with a certain line. That line led me to a character and a situation I was suddenly invested in. But I was still resisting a bit. Another graduate student said something I have never forgotten: "This is fine, but it would be so much better if you would lose the punch line at the end." She was right. I was not quite ready to take something from an exercise and make it matter. But given the choice between an OK joke and a good story, well, I chose the story. "Radioman" was the first story I completed for my collection.

Brian Kiteley: What other methods have you discovered when you've used exercises in your workshops?

Janet Bland: I like students to see what different people can do with the same exercise. Workshops are not just for letting other folks read one's own brilliant fiction. They are also for getting to see how others work. When I assign a section of exercises, like Characters from *The 3 A.M. Epiphany*, I say the students can choose among the exercises. But often there are overlaps, and we end up discussing two or three versions of the same exercise. Students immediately comment on the diversity of response to the same task, and the varying levels of success. Subtleties of style and voice are revealed, but even more so, students begin to consider the multiplicity of tasks that go into writing a short story. It doesn't take long for students to begin to identify their own strengths and weaknesses of craft. From here we are open to discussions of creative process, the imbedded tensions between narrative intent and results on the page, and how to learn from other writers and develop voice. Just as I hope my students get used to a variety of responses from readers, I want them to see that a workshop can be, at its best, a creative community, a way to learn and grow together as young writers.

I have often encouraged my students to hang on to your book, to reconsider exercises they felt were unsuccessful and to try new ones. I would like to imagine they could keep writing exercises on their own. Although it's not uncommon for students to tell me that they are still using the book after the workshop has ended, I never know how they might be using it. As you compiled these exercises, did you ever think of your book as something a writer could use while not in a workshop? I can see it as the basis of a writing group or creative community formed outside of academia, or even in the absence of a writing group, but I am wondering if all your intentions were based in the workshop.

Brian Kiteley: It took me a long while to wrap my mind around the idea that this book might also be useful outside fiction workshops. My editor (of *The 3 A.M. Epiphany*) Michelle Ehrhard and my agent Laurie Marcus-Wade both worked with me to broaden the language I used in the manuscript of the book, to make it more accessible to writers who were not in a university setting. I've also taken the exercises to a couple of high school classes, over the years, and it was refreshing to see how they worked in that slightly different setting. Since it's been published, I have gotten a lot of e-mails from people who are part of writers' groups. I am happy to see that the book travels well. It is not anti-intellectual (a nice double negative). I talk about philosophers, difficult writers, the science of consciousness—things I thought might irritate a general audience. That doesn't seem to have happened.

EXERCISE
INDEX

Abalone. 243

Abandonment 222

Addicted to Love. 109

After Auschwitz. 190

Alcohol 244

Ambition. 204

An American in Mecca 159

American Ramadan. 154

Among Schoolchildren 229

Anagrams 81

The Apocalypse 158

Aphorisms. 93

Autism 124

Automatic Writing. 88

Bacon in Egypt 245

A Beautiful Woman. 201

Beauty & Lust. 106

Beverly Sills 77

Big Two-Hearted River. 46

Biggar. 237

Biography of a Country 241

Birth Order. 221

Blind. 122

Blogs. 68

Boys & Girls. 233

Brothers 220

Bruno Schulz 49

A Burglar Smoking a Fine
    Cigar. 209

Buzzing Blooming Confusion . . 117

Camouflage. 163

The Camp 252

A Canticle for Leibowitz 46

A Car Wreck in Repose. 213

The Carnal & the Domestic. . . 103

Carrying a Body 148

Cartoon Texts 185

CBGB 195

Child Abuse 223

Christmas Every Three
    Months 195

Class Dismissed 250

Close Talker 205

Coincidence 95

The Collector of Injustices . . . 137

College 228

The Coma 149

Comic Balloons. 186

The Concept Album 78

Concordance. 82

Controlled Incongruity 182

Corporation vs. the Individual 249

Costumes 206

Country Noises 94

A Curse. 140

Daydreams 233

The Devil's Holiday 155

The Devious Lie of a Snapshot . 73

Divorce Sex. 114

Donald Rumsfeld 214

Doubt 174

Dressing Up 215

Driving 126

The Dust Bowl 192

Dying Young. 152

Encyclopedias 84

Enjoy the Process 133

Essay Fiction 38

Etymologies 31

Eunuch. 191

Fact and Fancy Reversed 91

Falling out of the Sky 148

The Fiction Writer & the
    Lawyer 202

Flâneur. 200

Fractured Fairy Tale. 210

Friendship's End 225

Friendships of the Good 223

Fruitfulness I. Kippers 207

The Fun in Funeral. 151

Good & Evil 177

Grace Paley 53

Grief. 133

Guy Walks Into a Bar 181

The Happy Boy and His
    Family. 71

On Hashish. 120

Headless Body in Topless Bar . 72

He's Had Enough 184

Hiding Emotions. 131

History & Fiction 193

History As Literary Looting . . 193

The Hotel Bed. 111

Ihab Hassan 48

The Impressionist 183

Information Sickness 118

The Insistence on Meaning. . . 116

Imagine Your Own Death 145

Index 88

Isaac Babel. 51

The Jean Cocteau Repertory. . 230

Killing the Parents 151

Language Is Always an
    Abbreviation 33

Laughter Is How We Connect. . 135

Learning to See. 121

The Letter A 34

The Letter B 35

The Letter in the Desk 227

Lies of the Press 70

Lobster Bisque 246

Lost. 240

Love & Chance. 108

Love E-mails. 114

Machine in the Garden 97

MapQuest 60

Marlon Brando 253

A Massacre 149

Meta-Humor. 179

Mirroring 234

Money 250

Multilingual 123

My Neighbor Totoro 63

Mythologizing Home 237

Naked City 241

Narcissism 125

Near Death 146

The Negative Master
Narrative 172

9/11 147

No Middle, Two Endings 92

No Time 52

Numerical Cognition 128

Obituary 143

Oddvertising 61

Old News 69

One Shit at a Time 172

Our Pets 226

Pain 130

Palimpsest 53

Paragraphs as Containers 31

Parataxis 29

Parents As Two Continents . . . 217

The Party 75

Perfect Weather 164

Philosophy and Its Discontents . . 98

Pillow Talk 112

The Pinup 65

Plants 211

Poetry & England 56

Potholes 35

Prep School 231

A Practical Joke 182

The Priest 157

Private Prayer 153

A Prospero Figure 198

Public Art 63

Recuperation 86

Recycling 96

Redness 132

Rejuveniles 207

Republicans 174

Reruns 65

Retinal Ennui 162

Rhetorical Questions 38

Ritual & Disorder 161

Robert Creeley 55

Selective Mutism 137

Self-Loathing 205

Serendipity 111

The Shouting Phase of Sitcoms . . 67

Siding With the Father 105

Sisters 220

Smell Is Emotional 167

Sobbing 136

Son of a Preacher Man 75

Song of Songs 102

Sorrow-Acre 40

The Story of a Year 190

Straight Man 187

Striptease 110

Substitution 87

Swearing. 249

Symbiosis 109

The Systems Novel 44

The Tarantula Hawk 169

Thanksgivings. 218

Therapeutic Lying. 213

That's Life. 166

The Three Stooges. 105

Translation from the Same
    Language. 86

Trialogue. 212

250 Different Words 85

UFO 165

Unbelieving 211

Unbelievers Exit Here 159

The United States & Canada. . 239

A U.S. Town 240

Wallace & Gromit. 199

War Stories 175

The Watchtower 158

We Think With the Objects
    We Love 139

Weekly Exercise. 90

What Democracy Means
    to Me. 170

Xenophobia. 150

Your Swann. 42

ABOUT THE AUTHOR

 Brian Kiteley is a professor in the creative writing program at the University of Denver (one of the very few schools to offer a Ph.D. in creative writing); he teaches writing workshops to both undergrads and grads. He has published two novels, *Still Life With Insects* (Ticknor & Fields, 1989) and *I Know Many Songs, But I Cannot Sing* (Simon & Schuster, 1996). His novel *The River Gods* will be published in the fall of 2009 by FC2. Awards include the Whiting Writers Award; a Guggenheim; and a Writing Fellowship with the NEA, 1991–92. His work has been published in *Best American Short Stories*.

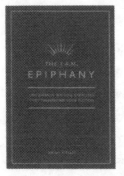

Printed in the United States
by Baker & Taylor Publisher Services